THE BOOK OF
Ice creams
& Sorbets

THE BOOK OF

Ice creams
& Sorbets

JACKI PASSMORE

Photography by PHILIP WYMANT

a Salamander book
Published by Salamander Books Limited
LONDON • NEW YORK

Published 1986 by Salamander Books Ltd.,
52 Bedford Row, London WC1R 4LR
By arrangement with Merehurst Press,
5 Great James Street, London WC1N 3DA
© Copyright Merehurst Limited 1986

Reprinted 1988

ISBN 0 86101 237 2

Editors: Susan Tomnay, Hilary Walden, Chris Fayers
Designers: Susan Kinealy, Roger Daniels, Richard Slater, Stuart Willard
Food stylist: Ann Creber
Photographer: Philip Wymant

Typeset by Lineage
Colour separation by New Interlitho S.p.A., Milan
Printed in Belgium by Proost International Book Production

Companion volumes of interest:
The Book of COCKTAILS
The Book of CHOCOLATES & PETITS FOURS
The Book of HORS D'OEUVRES
The Book of GARNISHES
The Book of PRESERVES
The Book of SAUCES
The Book of GIFTS FROM THE PANTRY
The Book of PASTA
The Book of HOT & SPICY NIBBLES – DIPS – DISHES
The Book of CRÊPES & OMELETTES
The Book of FONDUES
The Book of BISCUITS
The Book of CHEESECAKES

Contents

Introduction

It is heartening to know that once again
'real' ice cream is being made and marketed
commercially. For years we had to contend
with the insult of the so called commercial
'ice creams' – insipid in flavour, always
oversweet, almost totally artificially
produced from ingredients which bore
little relation to the actual components of a
good ice cream.
Ice cream, and fruit sorbets, can once again
be enjoyed by adults of discerning palate.
But, there is still nothing to compare with
the reward of preparing something
yourself. Ice creams use fresh dairy
products and real flavours; sorbets are
packed full of fresh fruit juices or purées.
Making ice creams and sorbets is not a
mysterious art. Home chefs have been
making them for centuries. And, it can be
done with an absolute minimum of
equipment. All you really need is a freezer
and a bit of determination. But, if you also
happen to be equipped with a food
processor or blender, and better still, an ice
cream churn or electric ice cream maker,
the task gets easier and easier.
However you undertake it, I know you
and your family will enjoy the results of
your labours!

Ice Creams

USE OF THE
MANUAL ICE CREAM CHURN

Manually operated ice cream churns consist of a bucket, usually made of slatted wood, with a metal container inside. A set of metal blades or paddles rotate inside the container when turned by an external handle. A mixture of crushed ice and rock salt is used to chill the ice; this mixture achieves lower temperatures than ice alone. It is packed firmly inside the bucket. Care must be taken that no salty liquid enters the metal container which holds the ice cream.

The salt is a coarse variety which may be available through speciality kitchen shops, speciality food shops, or larger food stores. The ice should be in small chips. Cubes or lumps of ice would fall through to the bottom making it ineffective as a freezing agent. Some ice dealers stock crushed party ice. If this is unobtainable, block ice can be chipped with an ice pick which resembles a spiked hammer. Or, you may crush cubed ice in a heavy bucket, using a sturdy rolling pin or a hammer.

When ice and salt are ready, the cooled custard, along with other ice cream or sorbet ingredients, are poured into the clean container. The lid is screwed firmly in place and the handle cranked. The ice cream or sorbet is ready when the handle offers firm resistance.

The ice cream or sorbet is churned by the rotation of the blades which stir the mixture continually, while scraping the sides and bottom of the container where the ice cream hardens first because of its contact with the cold metal.

When the ice cream or sorbet is ready, the container should be removed, ensuring that no drops of salt water fall in the container. Wipe the container, transfer contents to a covered container for freezing.

Ice cream can be served straight from the churn, but will be softer and have less flavour than if transferred to a freezer to 'develop'. Sorbets too will be soft, but are ready to serve if enjoyed that way.

ELECTRIC ICE CREAM CHURNS

There are several kinds of electric ice cream churns. A simple to use type can be placed within the freezer and requires no salt and ice. Another has an electrically operated churning action, and requires the same ice and salt preparation as does a manual churn.

The ultimate, though expensive, is the automatic freezer/churner ice cream maker. I enjoyed using an Italian–made automatic ice cream maker during the testing of these recipes; and, it has been in frequent use since, such is its ease of operation.

Required is a precooling period of five to six minutes to speed the freezing process before the ice cream or sorbet ingredients are added. The machine is switched on to CHURN and the ice cream is churned and frozen for the preset time. After the churning ceases the freezer continues to cool the ice cream.

Churning time is approximately 20 minutes and the ice cream will require a further 20 to 30 minutes in the machine to harden. Sorbets and ice creams made this way can be served straight from the machine.

CARE OF ICE CREAM MACHINES

Wooden churns, either manual or electric, should be washed thoroughly and left to dry before storage. The metal container, lid and paddles can be thoroughly washed with hot water and detergent, then rinsed with boiling water and dried well before being put away.

If a wooden churn has not been used for some time, it may have shrunk so that it is no longer watertight. Soak in cold water for a few hours and the wood will expand again.

Automatic electric ice cream makers are easy to clean. After use, rinse out the bowl several times with hot water. Wipe dry with a clean cloth. Thoroughly wash and dry blades and lid before storing.

DEVELOPING TIME

Cream and milk-based ice creams require a development time in order to be at their best. Allow at least one hour from time the ice cream has hardened for texture to set and flavours to fully develop. This extra time is not required for sorbets. Sorbets are best immediately they are made.

Ice creams made in an ice cream maker or churn can be served straight from the machine once they have firmed up completely, but again will be at their best if transferred to a freezer for 1 hour before serving.

STORAGE

Ice creams keep well if tightly covered. Plastic containers with press-in-place lids are ideal. Uncovered, ice creams become tainted and develop an unpleasant 'buttery' taste.

ON A PRACTICAL NOTE

Using up egg whites
Most of these ice cream recipes require egg yolks, which means you may be accumulating egg whites. For practicality, as well as to provide interesting ice cream accompaniments, included are a few recipes in the section on Cups, Decorations and Sauces, pages 105-123, utilising egg whites. Egg whites are ingredients in some ice cream and sorbet recipes. Egg whites can be refrigerated in a covered container for up to 1 week without spoiling. They freeze well. Make sure that no ice particles drip into the egg whites as this may prevent whisking up lightly and voluminously, which is especially important when making meringue.

Vanilla essence
Where vanilla extract is used, no specific amount has been given. This is because usually a few drops are sufficient. But remember that freezing deadens flavours so add a little more than you would normally use.

Scalding
In many of the ice cream recipes, the milk is 'scalded'. It should not reach a boil, but should be heated until small bubbles appear around the side of the saucepan.

Substituting honey for sugar
In many of the ice cream recipes, honey can be very successfully substituted for sugar. It should preferably be used where it does not overpower the other flavouring ingredients. Honey requires slightly longer to freeze than sugar, but has much the same sweetening quality.

EGG-BASED ICE CREAMS

There are 2 different ways of making ice creams based on eggs.

The classic creamy, rich ice cream, generally known as French Vanilla, is based on a cooked custard of egg yolks, sugar and cream. It is made in a way similar to that used to make a 'crème anglaise'.

This custard is used as the base for a variety of flavoured ice creams by adding the required ingredient – chocolate, praline, coffee, chopped nuts, fruit purée or liqueurs.

More economically, the same method can be applied, using fewer eggs and substituting milk or a mixture of milk and cream or pure cream. This produces a lighter, less creamy ice cream with fewer kilojoules (calories).

Eggs and sugar are beaten together into a smooth and homogeneous mass. Scalded cream is added and the mixture stirred over gentle heat until the custard slightly thickens. It is then cooled before being frozen or churned.

PARFAIT ICES

Parfait-style ice creams, while using significantly more eggs, are made by a completely different method and are feather-light and creamy concoctions. Either stiffly whisked egg whites for the lighter coloured or plain vanilla-flavoured parfaits, or well beaten egg yolks for coloured or strongly flavoured parfaits, are used. A boiling sugar syrup, cooked to just below the stage of colouring and caramelizing, is slowly poured over the eggs and vigorously beaten into the mixture. The heat partially cooks the eggs and the mixture becomes voluminous and very creamy. Cream, either whipped or unwhipped, is then folded through the eggs before freezing or churning.

OTHER ICE CREAM METHODS

Over the years a variety of different methods for making ice cream have been created, either out of economic necessity or to use ingredients on hand. Evaporated milk, condensed milk, egg whites, skimmed milk and yogurt are used to produce different tastes and styles of ice cream. I am particularly fond of frozen yogurt desserts. Yogurt is the ideal dessert alternative for those who are watching the calories or cholesterol. Plain yogurt flavoured with fruit purées, honey or carob achieves the same full-bodied taste and smooth texture of a custard-based ice cream, if somewhat firmer.

I have included two frozen yogurt ice cream recipes in this book. Use your imagination to create other flavours.

——— French Vanilla Ice Cream ———

*This type of custard ice cream churned in an ice cream maker will
have more volume than when beaten by hand.
Excellent ice cream can be produced by hand. It requires more work,
and the ice cream is slightly firmer in texture.*

*4 egg yolks
75g (2½ oz./⅓ cup) sugar
375 ml (12 fl. oz./1½ cups) single (light) cream
Vanilla essence to taste
Small pinch of salt*

In a medium stainless steel or heat-proof glass bowl or the top of a double saucepan, whisk the egg yolks and sugar until mixture is light, thick and smooth. A ribbon should form when beaters are lifted and drawn over surface of mixture.

In a small saucepan scald cream. Stir in vanilla and salt. Pour over eggs; mix well.

Place bowl or top of double saucepan over a pan of simmering water. Using a wooden spoon, stir slowly and continually 12 minutes until custard is thick enough to coat back of spoon. Do not allow water to boil.

Serving suggestion: Banana Split, page 125

Remove from heat. Set bowl in cold water. Cool to room temperature. Pour into ice cream container. Freeze in ice cream maker according to manufacturer's directions.

FREEZER METHOD: Pour prepared mixture into several undivided ice trays; cover; freeze until firm, 3 to 6 hours, place in freezer.

Using a fork, beat 3 to 4 times while freezing. Before serving refrigerate for 20 minutes to soften. Store in a covered container.

Makes 4 to 6 servings.

— *Economy Vanilla Ice Cream* —

3 egg yolks
125 g (4 oz./½ cup) sugar
500 ml (16 fl. oz./2 cups) milk
Vanilla essence to taste
To Garnish:
Sugared Flowers, page 114, if desired

In a stainless steel or heatproof glass bowl or the top of a double saucepan, whisk the egg yolks and sugar together until thick and creamy.

In a saucepan scald 250 ml (8 fl. oz./1 cup) milk; add vanilla; pour over the eggs, mix well. Stir slowly and continually over a saucepan of simmering water until thickened slightly, about 10 minutes. Remove from heat, pour in remaining milk, cool. Pour into ice cream container. Freeze in ice cream maker according to manufacturer's directions.

FREEZER METHOD: Pour prepared mixture into several undivided ice trays; cover, place in freezer; freeze until firm, 3-6 hours. Using a fork beat 3 to 4 times while freezing. Leave at least one hour for the flavour to develop.

Before serving, refrigerate 10 minutes to soften.

Garnish with Sugared Flowers if desired.

Makes 4-6 servings.

— *Chocolate Supreme Ice Cream* —

*60 g (2 oz.) plain (dark) chocolate pieces, broken into small
pieces
4 egg yolks
50 g (1¾ oz./¼ cup) sugar
Very small pinch of salt
375 ml (12 fl. oz./1½ cups) single (light) cream
Vanilla essence to taste
To Garnish:
Chocolate Caraque, page 113, if desired*

In a bowl over a saucepan of simmering water melt chocolate.

In a stainless steel or heatproof glass bowl or the top of a double
saucepan off the heat, whisk egg yolks, sugar and salt until thick and
creamy. In a medium saucepan scald cream, pour over eggs. Slowly
and continually stir custard over gently simmering water until
thickened slightly. Stir in chocolate, mix well. Cool. Pour into ice
cream container. Freeze in ice cream maker according to
manufacturer's directions.

FREEZER METHOD: Pour into several undivided ice trays, cover,
place in freezer, freeze until firm, 3 to 6 hours. Using a fork beat 3 to
4 times while freezing.

Before serving refrigerate at least 20 minutes to soften.

Garnish with Chocolate Caraque, if desired.

Makes 4-6 servings.

VARIATION:
White Chocolate Ice Cream: Substitute white chocolate pieces for the
plain chocolate and use a little extra vanilla essence.

Chocolate Ice Cream

3 egg yolks
185 g (6 oz./³⁄4 cup) sugar
500 ml (16 fl. oz./2 cups) milk
60 g (2 oz./1½ cup) cocoa or unsweetened carob powder
250 ml (8 fl.oz/1 cup) single (light) cream
Vanilla essence to taste

To Garnish:
Chocolate Leaves, page 112, if desired

In a stainless steel bowl or top of a double saucepan, whisk egg yolks and sugar until light and creamy.

In a small saucepan, scald milk. Stir in cocoa or carob powder; mix thoroughly. Pour over eggs. Place bowl or top of double saucepan over a pan of simmering water. Stir slowly and continually 10 minutes or until custard slightly thickens.

Remove from heat. Stir in cream and vanilla; cool. Pour into ice cream container. Freeze in ice cream maker according to manufacturer's directions.

FREEZER METHOD: Pour prepared mixture in several undivided ice trays; cover; place in freezer; freeze until firm, 3 to 6 hours. Using a fork stir 3 to 4 times while freezing. Store in a covered container. Before serving, refrigerate 20 minutes to soften. Garnish with Chocolate Leaves, if desired.

Makes 6 to 8 servings.

VARIATION:
Mocca Ice Cream: Add 1 tablespoon instant coffee powder to milk when preparing custard. Or add 2 tablespoons coffee liqueur to prepared custard before freezing.

Praline Ice Cream

This light ice cream highlights the crisp nuttiness of praline.

4 egg yolks
50 g (1¾ oz./¼ cup) sugar
185 ml (6 fl. oz./¾ cup) milk
185 ml (6 fl. oz./¾ cup) single (light) cream
Vanilla essence to taste
½ cup praline, page 110
Orange slices, if desired
Biscuits, if desired

To Garnish:
Mint Leaves, if desired

In a stainless steel bowl or top of a double saucepan, whisk egg yolks and sugar until thick.

In a small saucepan, scald milk. Pour over eggs. Place bowl or top of double boiler over a pan of simmering water. Stir slowly and continually 10 minutes or until custard thickens. Remove from heat. Stir in cream and vanilla.

Stir in praline; cool. Pour into ice cream canister. Freeze in ice cream maker according to manufacturer's directions.

FREEZER METHOD: Pour prepared mixture in several undivided ice trays; cover; place in freezer; freeze until firm, 3 to 6 hours. Using a fork beat 3 to 4 times while freezing. Store in a covered container. Serve with orange slices and a biscuit, if desired. Garnish with mint leaves, if desired.

Makes 4 to 6 servings.

Coffee Praline Ice Cream

4 egg yolks
50 g (1¾ oz./¼ cup) sugar
250 ml (8 fl. oz./1 cup) milk
2 tablespoons instant coffee powder
500 ml (16 fl. oz./2 cups) whipping cream
185 g (6 oz./¾ cup) praline, page 110
Biscuits, if desired

To Garnish:
Crushed praline, if desired

In a stainless steel bowl or top of a double saucepan, whisk egg yolks and sugar until smooth and creamy. In a small saucepan, scald milk; stir in coffee powder. Pour over eggs. Place bowl or top of double saucepan over a pan of simmering water. Stir slowly and continually 10 minutes or until custard thickens. Remove from heat; cool. Stir in cream.

Pour into ice cream container. Freeze in ice cream maker according to manufacturer's directions. Add praline just before ice cream firmly freezes.

FREEZER METHOD: In a medium bowl, whip cream to soft peaks. Stir in praline. Fold into cooled custard. Pour into several undivided ice trays; cover; place in freezer; freeze until firm, 3 to 6 hours. Using a fork beat once while freezing. Store in a covered container. Serve with a biscuit, if desired.

Garnish with crushed praline, if desired.

Makes 6 servings.

VARIATION:
Line small custard cups with plastic wrap. Fill with coffee praline ice cream. Freeze until firm. Unmould on dessert plates; surround with Vanilla Cream Sauce, page 117.

Caramel Ice Cream

6 egg yolks
220 g (7 oz./1 cup) sugar
500 ml (16 fl. oz./2 cups) milk
250 ml (8 fl. oz./1 cup) single (light) cream
Vanilla essence to taste
Biscuits, if desired

To Garnish:
Chocolate Leaves, page 112, if desired

In a stainless steel bowl or top of a double saucepan, whisk egg yolks and 90 g (3 oz./⅓ cup) sugar until thick and creamy. In a small saucepan, scald milk. Pour over eggs. Place bowl or top of double saucepan over a pan of simmering water. Stir slowly and continually 10 minutes or until custard slightly thickens.

In a small saucepan, cook remaining sugar over low heat until a golden brown. Remove from heat; stir in cream and vanilla essence until well mixed. Pour caramel into custard; stir until caramel is dissolved. Cool. Pour into ice cream container. Freeze in ice cream maker according to manufacturer's directions.

FREEZER METHOD: Pour prepared mixture into several undivided ice trays; cover; place in freezer; freeze until firm, 3 to 6 hours. Using a fork, beat 3 to 4 times while freezing. Store in a covered container.

Serve with biscuits, if desired.

Garnish with Chocolate Leaves, if desired.

Makes 6-8 servings.

VARIATION:
Caramel Crunch Ice Cream: In a small saucepan, caramelize 105 g (3½ oz./½ cup) sugar over low heat until golden brown. Pour onto oiled plate. Let set until hard. Break in small pieces.

Fold in caramel just before ice cream firms. Freeze. Or sprinkle over top of ice cream before serving.

Butterscotch Ice Cream

105 g (3½ oz./½ cup) sugar
1 tablespoon water
90 ml (3 fl. oz./⅓ cup) golden syrup
500 ml (16 fl. oz./2 cups) whipping cream
4 egg yolks
Vanilla essence to taste
Meringue cases, page 107
Biscuits, if desired

TO GARNISH:
Broken Toffee, if desired

In a small thick saucepan, cook sugar and water over a low heat until sugar dissolves; boil until dark golden brown. Quickly beat in syrup and 90 ml (3 fl. oz./⅓ cup) cream.

In a stainless steel or heatproof glass bowl, whisk egg yolks until creamy. Drizzle hot butterscotch over eggs; beat vigorously until mixture is smooth, thick and cool.

In a small bowl, mix remaining cream with vanilla. Pour butterscotch mixture and cream into ice cream container. Freeze in ice cream maker according to manufacturer's directions.

FREEZER METHOD: In a small bowl, whip remaining cream with vanilla. Fold into butterscotch mixture. Pour mixture into several undivided ice trays; cover; place in freezer. Freeze until firm; 3 to 6 hours. Store in covered container. Serve in a meringue with a biscuit, if desired. Garnish with broken toffee, if desired.

Makes 4 to 6 servings.

VARIATIONS:
Butterscotch Brickle: Grease a plate and a small saucepan, cook 60 g (2 oz./¼ cup) sugar with 1 teaspoon water until fully golden brown. Stir in 2 teaspoons golden syrup and 1 teaspoon of butter or margarine. Pour on prepared plate to harden.

Break up toffee; add just before ice cream is firmly frozen.

Spicy Vanilla Ice Cream

SPICED MILK:
250 ml (8 fl. oz./1 cup) milk
1 cinnamon stick
2 whole green cardamoms, broken
2 cm (¾in) fresh ginger root piece, peeled and crushed
4 whole cloves
½ teaspoon ground cinnamon
½ teaspoon freshly grated nutmeg

CUSTARD:
4 egg yolks
105 g (3½ oz./½ cup) sugar
375 ml (12 fl. oz./1½ cups) single (light) cream
Vanilla essence to taste

TO GARNISH:
Chocolate Caraque, page 113, if desired
Powdered cinnamon, if desired

In a small saucepan, simmer milk with spices 30 minutes. Remove from heat; let stand, covered, until cool. Strain through a fine nylon sieve.

In a stainless steel bowl or top of a double boiler, whisk egg yolks and sugar until thick and creamy.

In a small saucepan, scald cream and strained milk with vanilla. Pour over eggs. Place bowl or top of double saucepan over a pan of simmering water. Stir slowly and continuously 10 minutes or until custard thickens.

Pour into ice cream canister. Freeze in ice cream maker according to manufacturer's directions.

FREEZER METHOD: Pour prepared mixture into several undivided ice trays; cover; place in freezer, freeze until firm, 3 to 6 hours. Using a fork, beat 3 to 4 times while freezing.

Store in covered container.

Before serving, refrigerate 20 minutes to soften.

Garnish with Chocolate Caraque, if desired.

Makes 4 to 6 servings.

Butterscotch Log

This is an interesting-looking dessert – a circle of creamy butterscotch ice cream rimmed with chocolate crumbs. It's especially popular with children.

Butterscotch Ice Cream, page 20
90 g (3 oz.) plain (dark) chocolate, chopped
2 tablespoons cocoa powder

TO GARNISH:
Chocolate Caraque, page 113, if desired

When ice cream is firmly frozen remove from tray. Place in centre of a piece of foil large enough to cover completely. Form into a log shape. Wrap tightly with foil. Freeze until very firm. In a food processor/blender, process chocolate and cocoa to fine crumbs.

Remove log from freezer; unwrap. Coat thickly with chocolate crumbs. To serve, cut into slices.

Garnish with Chocolate Caraque, if desired.

Makes 6 servings.

Honey Ice Cream

The flavour of honey used will dominate this ice cream. (See general note on using honey in ice creams, page 10).

2 egg yolks
1 egg white
Small pinch of salt
375 ml (12 fl. oz./1½ cups) milk
250 g (8 oz./¾ cup) honey
250 ml (8 fl. oz./1 cup) single (light) cream
Honey, if desired

To Garnish:
Biscuit, if desired
Sugared Fruit and Leaves, page 114, if desired

In a stainless steel bowl or top of a double saucepan whisk egg yolks, egg white and salt until smooth. In a small saucepan, scald milk; blend in honey. Pour over eggs. Place bowl or top of double saucepan over a pan of simmering water. Stir slowly and continually until custard slightly thickens.

Remove from heat. Stir in cream; cool.

Pour into ice cream container. Freeze in ice cream maker according to manufacturer's directions.

FREEZER METHOD: Pour prepared mixture into several undivided ice trays; cover; place in freezer and freeze until firm, 3 to 6 hours. Using a fork, beat twice.

Store in covered container.

Before serving refrigerate 15 minutes to soften.

Serve over honey, if desired.

Garnish with biscuits and Sugared Fruit and Leaves, if desired.

Makes 6 servings.

— Rum and Hazelnut Ice Cream —

3 egg yolks
105 g (3½ oz./½ cup) sugar
250 ml (8 fl. oz./1 cup) milk
375 ml (12 fl. oz./1½ cups) single (light) cream
Vanilla essence to taste
60 ml (2 fl. oz./¼ cup) dark rum
60 g (2 oz./½ cup) hazelnuts, toasted, coarsely chopped
Biscuits, if desired

In the top of a double saucepan, whisk egg yolks and sugar until thick and creamy.

In a small saucepan, scald milk. Pour over eggs. Place liquid in double saucepan over a pan of simmering water. Stir slowly and continually until custard thickens. Stir in cream and vanilla; cool.

Pour custard and rum into ice cream container. Freeze in ice cream maker according to manufacturer's directions. Fold in nuts just before ice cream firmly freezes.

FREEZER METHOD: Stir rum into custard. Pour mixture into several undivided ice trays; cover; place in freezer; freeze until firm, 3 to 6 hours. Using a fork, beat twice while freezing. Fold in nuts just before ice cream firmly freezes.

Store in covered container.

Serve with biscuits, if desired.

Makes 6 servings.

— Rum and Raisin Ice Cream —

155 g (5 oz./1 cup) raisins
185 ml (6 fl. oz./³/4 cup) dark rum
4 egg yolks
50 g (1³/4 oz./¹/4 cup) sugar
250 ml (8 fl. oz./1 cup) milk
375 ml (12 fl. oz./1¹/2 cups) whipping cream
Vanilla essence to taste
Fresh grapes, if desired

In a small bowl, combine raisins and rum, let stand 3 to 4 hours.

In a stainless steel bowl or top of a double saucepan, whisk egg yolks and sugar until light, thick and creamy.

In a small saucepan, scald milk. Pour over eggs; mix well.

Place stainless steel bowl or top of double saucepan over a pan of simmering water. Stir slowly and continually 10 minutes or until custard slightly thickens.

Drain raisins. Add rum to custard; cool. Pour custard, cream and vanilla into ice cream container. Freeze in ice cream maker according to manufacturer's directions. Fold in raisins just before ice cream firmly freezes.

FREEZER METHOD: Whip cream and vanilla to soft peaks. Fold into custard. Pour prepared mixture into several undivided ice trays; cover; place in freezer; freeze until firm, 3 to 6 hours. Using fork, beat 3 to 4 times while freezing. Add raisins just before ice cream firmly freezes.

Store in a covered container.

Serve with grapes, if desired.

Makes 6 to 8 servings.

Fruit Salad and Cream Ice Cream

280 g (9 oz./2 cups) fresh or canned fruit salad, drained,
chopped
2 tablespoons Maraschino or brandy
3 egg yolks
50 g (1¾ oz./¼ cup) sugar
500 ml (16 fl. oz./2 cups) milk
Vanilla essence to taste
500 ml (16 fl. oz./2 cups) whipped cream

TO GARNISH:
Fresh fruit, if desired
Mint leaves, if desired

In a small bowl, combine fruit salad and Maraschino or brandy, let stand 2 hours.

In a stainless steel bowl or top of a double saucepan, whisk egg yolks and sugar until thick and creamy.

In a small saucepan, scald milk. Pour over eggs. Place bowl or top of double boiler over a pan of simmering water. Stir slowly and continually 10 minutes or until custard thickens slightly. Add vanilla; cool. Stir fruit salad into custard.

Pour into ice cream container. Freeze in ice cream maker according to manufacturer's directions.

When ready, smooth the top of the ice cream. Spread whipped cream over Fruit Salad Ice Cream. Place in freezer; freeze until firm.

FREEZER METHOD: Pour mixture into several undivided ice trays; cover; place in freezer; freeze until firm, 3 to 6 hours. Using a fork, beat 3 times while freezing. Spread whipped cream over Fruit Salad Ice Cream. Freeze until firm.

Store in a covered container.

Garnish with fruit and mint leaves, if desired.

Makes 6 to 8 servings.

Fruit and Nut Ice Cream

60 g (2 oz./½ cup) mixed nuts, toasted, coarsely chopped
155 g (5 oz./1 cup) mixed dried fruit
75 ml (2½ fl. oz./⅓ cup) cognac or brandy
60 ml (2 fl. oz./⅓ cup) sugar syrup, page 64 (or 50 g (1¾
oz./¼ cup) sugar and a little water)
3 egg yolks
2 tablespoons sugar
Small pinch of salt
375 ml (12 fl. oz./1½ cups) milk
Vanilla essence to taste

TO GARNISH:
Nuts, if desired
Chopped crystallized fruit, if desired

In a small bowl, combine nuts, fruit, cognac or brandy and sugar syrup. Cover with cling film; let stand 2 hours.

In a stainless steel bowl or top of a double saucepan, whisk egg yolks and sugar until light, thick and smooth.

In a small saucepan, add salt to milk; scald. Pour over eggs; mix well. Place bowl or top of double saucepan over a pan of simmering water. Stir slowly and continually 10 minutes or until custard thickens slightly; cool.

Pour into ice cream container. Freeze in ice cream maker according to manufacturer's directions. Fold in fruit and nut mixture with vanilla when ice cream is beginning to firm.

FREEZER METHOD: Fold fruit and nut mixture with vanilla into cooled custard. Pour mixture into several undivided ice trays; cover; place in freezer; freeze until firm, 3 to 6 hours. Using a fork beat 3 to 4 times while freezing.

Before serving, refrigerate briefly to soften.

Store in a covered container.

Garnish with nuts and crystallized fruit, if desired.

Makes 4 to 6 servings.

– *Fruit and Nut Chocolate Bombe* –

Ice Cream Christmas Pudding
In those southern countries where Christmas Day falls in summer,
traditional hot Christmas Pudding is often too rich and heavy to be really
enjoyed. This creamy and delicious bombe makes a fine alternative.

Fruit and Nut Ice Cream, page 27
Chocolate Ice Cream, page 16
Rum Sauce, page 119, or Rich Brandy Sauce, page 118

To Garnish:
Maraschino cherries, if desired

Line a bombe mould or a pudding basin with cling film. Using a spoon dipped in cold water, spread Chocolate Ice Cream in a thick layer around sides and bottom, then fill centre with Fruit and Nut Ice Cream.

Cover; place in freezer, freeze until very firm.

To serve, unmould onto a serving plate. Slice in wedges. Serve with sauce.

Garnish with cherries, if desired.

Makes 8 to 10 servings.

— *Muesli and Honey Ice Cream* —

A crunchy toasted muesli, accentuated with dried fruits, desiccated coconut and whole almonds and hazelnuts, gives this healthful ice cream a unique taste.

250 g (8 oz./¾ cup) honey
4 eggs, separated
Salt
500 ml (16 fl. oz./2 cups) whipping cream
Vanilla essence to taste
125 g (4 oz./1 cup) toasted muesli with fruit and nuts
Crisp Ice Cream Cases, page 106, if desired

In a medium bowl, whisk honey, egg yolks and a small pinch of salt until creamy.

In a medium bowl, whip cream and vanilla to soft peaks. Fold into honey mixture. Mix in muesli.

In a small bowl, whisk egg whites and a small pinch of salt to stiff peaks. Fold in honey mixture. Pour prepared mixture into several undivided ice trays; cover; place in freezer; freeze until firm, 3 to 6 hours. Using a fork, stir once while freezing. This ice cream remains fairly soft.

Serve in Crisp Ice Cream Cases, if desired.

Makes 8 servings.

VARIATION:
Honey and Coconut Ice Cream: Substitute toasted desiccated coconut for muesli.

Pistachio Nut Ice Cream

3 egg yolks
185 g (6 oz./³⁄₄ cup) sugar
Vanilla essence to taste
500 ml (16 fl. oz./2 cups) single (light) cream
Green food colouring, if desired
125 g (4 oz./1 cup) chopped pistachio nuts

TO GARNISH:
Biscuits, if desired
Chopped pistachio nuts, if desired

In a stainless steel bowl or top of a double saucepan, whisk egg yolks, sugar and vanilla until thick and creamy.

In a small saucepan, scald ½ of cream. Stir into eggs. Place bowl or top of double saucepan over a pan of simmering water. Using a wooden spoon, stir slowly and continually until custard is thick enough to coat back of spoon. Remove from heat; cool. Pour custard, remaining cream, and food colouring, if desired, into ice cream container. Freeze in ice cream maker according to manufacturer's directions. Fold in nuts just before ice cream firmly freezes.

FREEZER METHOD: Stir remaining cream, nuts and food colouring, if desired, into custard. Pour prepared mixture into several undivided ice trays. Cover; place in freezer; freeze until firm, 3 to 6 hours. Using a fork, beat twice while freezing.

Store in a covered container.

Serve with a biscuit, if desired.

Garnish with chopped pistachio nuts, if desired.

Makes 6 servings.

—— *Creamy Pecan Ice Cream* ——

2 egg yolks
1 whole egg
185 g (6 oz./³/4 cup) sugar
Vanilla essence to taste
500 ml (16 fl. oz./2 cups) single (light) cream
125 g (4 oz./1 cup) chopped pecans, walnuts, hazelnuts or
pistachio nuts
Spun Sugar, page 108, if desired

TO GARNISH:
Chopped pecans, walnuts or hazelnuts, if desired

In a stainless steel bowl or top of a double saucepan, whisk egg
yolks, whole egg and sugar until creamy. Add vanilla. In a small
saucepan, scald ½ of cream. Add to egg mixture. Place bowl or top
of double saucepan over a pan of simmering water. Stir slowly and
continually until custard is thick enough to coat back of the spoon.
Remove from heat. Mix in remaining cream.

Pour into ice cream container. Freeze according to manufacturer's
directions.

When ice cream is almost firm, fold in nuts. Freeze until firm.

FREEZER METHOD: Add nuts to custard mixture. Pour prepared
mixture into several undivided ice trays; cover; place in freezer;
freeze until firm, 3 to 6 hours. Using a fork, beat twice while
freezing.

Store in a covered container. Serve in a nest of Spun Sugar, if desired.
Garnish with chopped pecans, walnuts or hazelnuts, if desired.

Makes 6 servings.

Peanut Butter Ice Cream

Crunchy peanut butter gives this ice cream a yummy nutty taste.

3 egg yolks
125 ml (4 oz./¹/₂ cup) sugar or honey
250 ml (8 fl. oz./1 cup) milk
250 g (8 oz./1 cup) crunchy peanut butter
Vanilla essence to taste
375 ml (12 fl. oz./1¹/₂ cups) whipping cream
Ice cream cones, if desired

To Garnish:
Chopped nuts
Peanut halves
Melted chocolate

In a small bowl, whisk egg yolks and sugar or honey until smooth and creamy.

In a stainless steel bowl or top of a double saucepan set over a pan of boiling water, heat milk. Reduce heat until water simmers.

Stir in egg mixture; whisk well. Stir slowly until custard slightly thickens. Remove from heat. Beat in peanut butter. Beat until cool. Stir in vanilla. Pour cream and custard into ice cream container. Freeze in ice cream maker according to manufacturer's directions.

FREEZER METHOD: In a small bowl, whip cream to soft peaks. Fold into custard. Pour prepared mixture into several undivided ice trays; cover; place in freezer; freeze until firm, 3 to 6 hours. Using a fork, stir 2 to 3 times while freezing.

Store in a covered container.

Serve in ice cream cones, if desired.

Garnish with chopped nuts, peanut halves and melted chocolate, if desired.

Makes 8 servings.

Kulfi (Indian Ice Cream)

Kulfi is traditionally set in cone-shaped lidded metal containers which are rubbed between the hands to warm and release the frozen treats.

950 ml (32 fl. oz./4 cups) milk
185 g (6 oz./³/4 cup) sugar
1 tablespoon cornflour
2 tablespoons sweetened condensed milk, if desired
Water or milk
2 tablespoons chopped pistachio nuts
2 tablespoons chopped almonds
2 teaspoons rose water or 1 to 2 green cardamon pods, cracked
Fresh fruit, if desired

To GARNISH:
Chopped nuts, if desired

In a small saucepan, reduce milk to ½ of original quantity. Add sugar; stir until dissolved. (If using cardamom pods add to milk before reducing. Remove before mixing in cornflour.)

Mix cornflour and condensed milk, if desired, with enough cold water or milk to make a thin paste. Stir in sweetened milk; pour back into pan. Cook over a low heat stirring until mixture slightly thickens. Remove from heat; cool.

Add nuts and rose water, if used. Pour prepared mixture into several undivided ice trays, cover, place in freezer, freeze until firm, 3 to 6 hours.

Store in a covered container.

Before serving, refrigerate 20 minutes to soften.

Serve with fresh fruit, if desired.

Garnish with chopped nuts, if desired.

Makes 6 servings.

— Old English Toffee Ice Cream —

This ice cream is made in two stages and then swirled together to give a marbled effect.

185 g (6 oz./¾ cup) sugar
5 egg yolks
685 ml (22 fl. oz./2¾ cups) single (light) cream
Vanilla essence to taste
Crisp Ice Cream Cases, page 106, if desired

In a small saucepan, cook 105 g (3½ oz./½ cup) sugar over low heat until a dark golden brown. In a stainless steel or heatproof bowl, whisk 3 egg yolks. Pour 250 ml (8 fl. oz./1 cup) cream into sugar. Stir to prevent boiling over. When cream is piping hot and caramel has completely melted, pour over eggs. Beat well; cool.

Pour into ice cream container. Freeze in ice cream maker according to manufacturer's directions. Transfer to a freezer container; cover; place in freezer.

In a stainless steel or heatproof bowl, whisk remaining sugar and egg yolks until thick and smooth. In a small saucepan, scald remaining cream. Add vanilla; pour over eggs. Place bowl over a pan of simmering water. Stir slowly and continually until custard coats back of spoon. Cool.

Repeat procedure for freezing in ice cream maker. Stir frozen ice creams together to get marbled effect.

FREEZER METHOD: Pour each prepared mixture into several undivided ice trays; cover; place in freezer; freeze until firm, 3 to 6 hours. Using a fork, beat twice while freezing. When firm, stir again using a fork. Mix ice creams together to give a marbled effect. Cover and refreeze.

Store in a covered container.
Serve in a Crisp Ice Cream Case, if desired.

Makes 6 servings.

Gooseberry Ice Cream

375 g (12 oz./2 cups) fresh or frozen gooseberries, topped
and tailed
60 ml (2 fl. oz./¼ cup) water
220 g (7 oz./1 cup) sugar
2 egg yolks
250 ml (8 fl. oz./1 cup) milk
250 ml (8 fl. oz./1 cup) cream
Vanilla essence to taste
Biscuits, if desired
Fresh gooseberries, if desired

In a small saucepan, combine gooseberries with water and ¼ of
sugar. Stir to dissolve sugar. Cover; cook over low heat until tender.
 Remove from heat; cool. In a food processor/blender, process fruit
and liquid to a purée.
 Strain through a fine nylon sieve, pressing with a wooden spoon.
Discard seeds and skins.
 In a stainless steel bowl or top of a double saucepan, whisk
remaining sugar and egg yolks until thick and smooth. In a small
saucepan, scald the milk. Pour over eggs. Place bowl or top of
double saucepan over a pan of simmering water. Stir slowly and
continually until custard slightly thickens. Remove from heat. Stir
in fruit purée, cream and vanilla.
 Pour into ice cream container. Freeze in an ice cream maker
according to manufacturer's directions.

FREEZER METHOD: Pour prepared mixture into several undivided
ice trays; cover; place in freezer; freeze until firm, 3 to 6 hours. Using
a fork, beat 2 to 3 times while freezing.
 Store in a covered container.
 Serve with a biscuit and gooseberries, if desired.

Makes 6 to 8 servings.

VARIATION:
Blackcurrant Ice Cream: Substitute blackcurrants for the gooseberries.

—— *Passionfruit Ice Cream (1)* ——

250 ml (8 fl. oz./1 cup) sweetened condensed milk
500 ml (16 fl. oz./2 cups) milk
185 ml (6 fl. oz./3/4 cup) passionfruit pulp (about 10 ripe
passionfruit)
Biscuits and Passionfruit Sauce, page 120, if desired

In a medium bowl, mix condensed milk and milk, stir in the passionfruit pulp. Pour into ice cream container. Freeze in ice cream maker according to manufacturer's directions.

FREEZER METHOD: Pour prepared mixture into several undivided ice trays; cover. Place in freezer; freeze until firm, 3 to 6 hours. Using a fork, beat every ½ hour while freezing. Store in a covered container.
Serve with a biscuit and Passionfruit Sauce, if desired.

Makes 6 servings.

VARIATION:
Passionfruit Parfait: In tall parfait glasses, layer scoops of Passionfruit and Vanilla Ice Cream, page 12-13. Drizzle Passionfruit Sauce over each. Cover with whipped cream and toasted flaked almonds. Decorate with a passionfruit flower or a wafer.

Passionfruit Ice Cream (2)

This recipe is based on traditional custard.

4 egg yolks
105 g (3½ oz./½ cup) sugar
500 ml (16 fl. oz./2 cups) milk
250 ml (8 fl. oz./1 cup) single (light) cream
250 ml (8 fl. oz./1 cup) passionfruit pulp (about 12 ripe passionfruit)
Biscuits and Passionfruit Sauce, page 120, if desired

In a stainless steel bowl or top of a double saucepan, whisk egg yolks and sugar until light and creamy.

In a small saucepan, scald milk. Pour over eggs. Place bowl or top of double saucepan over a pan of simmering water. Stir slowly and continually 10 minutes or until custard slightly thickens.

Pour custard, cream and passionfruit into ice cream container. Freeze in ice cream maker according to manufacturer's directions.

FREEZER METHOD: Fold cream and passionfruit pulp into custard. Pour mixture into several undivided ice trays; cover; place in freezer; freeze until firm, 3 to 6 hours. Using a fork, beat every ½ hour 3 to 4 times while freezing.

Store in covered container. Before serving refrigerate 20 minutes to soften.

Serve with a biscuit and Passionfruit Sauce, if desired.

Makes 6 to 8 servings.

Apricot Ice Cream

125 g (4 oz./²/₃ cup) dried apricots
3 egg yolks
220 g (7 oz./1 cup) sugar
250 ml (8 fl. oz./1 cup) milk
250 ml (8 fl. oz./1 cup) single (light) cream

To Garnish:
Crystallized apricots, if desired
Mint leaves, if desired

In a small saucepan, cover apricots with cold water. Cook over medium heat until very tender; cool. In a food processor/blender, process apricots and cooking liquid to a smooth purée.

In a stainless steel bowl or top of a double saucepan, whisk egg yolks and sugar until thick and creamy.

In a small saucepan, scald milk and cream. Pour over eggs. Place bowl or top of double saucepan over a pan of simmering water. Stir slowly and continually 10 minutes or until custard is creamy. Remove from heat; cool. Pour custard and puréed apricots into ice cream container. Freeze in ice cream maker according to manufacturer's directions.

FREEZER METHOD: Stir puréed apricots into custard; cool. Pour mixture into several undivided ice trays; cover; place in freezer; freeze until firm, 3 to 6 hours. Using a fork, beat every ½ hour 3 to 4 times.

Store in a covered container.

Before serving, refrigerate 20 minutes to soften.

Garnish with crystallized apricots and a mint leaf, if desired.

Makes 6 servings.

Papaya and Passionfruit Ice Cream

4 egg yolks
105 g (3½ oz./½ cup) sugar
250 ml (8 fl. oz./1 cup) milk
250 ml (8 fl. oz./1 cup) single (light) cream
315 g (10 oz./2 cups) fresh or drained canned papaya, diced
60 ml (2 fl. oz./⅓ cup) passionfruit pulp (about 4 passionfruit)
Biscuits and Passionfruit Sauce, page 120

In a stainless steel bowl or top of a double saucepan, whisk egg yolks and sugar until thick and light.

In a small saucepan, scald milk. Pour over eggs, place bowl or top of double saucepan over a pan of simmering water. Using a wooden spoon, stir slowly and continually until custard thickens enough to coat back of spoon. Remove from heat. Add cream; cool.

In a food processor/blender, process papaya into a smooth purée.

Pour custard, papaya purée and passionfruit pulp into ice cream container. Freeze in ice cream maker according to manufacturer's directions.

FREEZER METHOD: Stir papaya purée and passionfruit pulp into custard. Pour mixture into several undivided ice trays; cover; place in freezer; freeze until almost firm. Using a fork, beat vigorously. Return to freezer, freeze until firm.

Serve with a biscuit and Passionfruit Sauce, if desired.

Makes 6 to 8 servings.

Pineapple Ice Cream

1 large pineapple, peeled, cored, cubed
Juice of 1 lime or lemon
75 g (2½ oz./⅓ cup) sugar
375 ml (12 fl. oz./1½ cups) whipping cream
Pineapple slices, if desired

To Garnish:
Mint leaves, if desired
Pineapple syrup, if desired

In a food processor/blender, process pineapple, lime or lemon juice and sugar to a thick purée. Pour mixture into several undivided ice trays. Place in freezer; beat to a slush.

In a small bowl, whip cream to soft peaks. Return pineapple to processor/blender; process until smooth. Pour pineapple into a medium bowl. Fold in cream. Pour again into ice trays; cover; place in freezer; freeze until firm, 3 to 6 hours.

Store in a covered container.

Before serving, refrigerate 20 minutes to soften.

Serve with pineapple slices, if desired.

Garnish with mint leaves and pineapple syrup.

Makes 8 servings.

Neapolitan Strawberry Ice Cream

500 g (1 lb./3 cups) fresh strawberries, mashed
105 g (3½ oz./½ cup) sugar
350 ml (12 fl. oz./1½ cups) whipping cream

To Garnish:
Fresh strawberries, if desired
Mint leaves, if desired

In a food processor/blender, process strawberries and sugar to a smooth purée. Pour strawberry purée and cream into ice cream container. Freeze in ice cream maker according to manufacturer's directions.

FREEZER METHOD: In a medium bowl, lightly whip cream. Fold in strawberry purée. Pour mixture into several undivided trays; cover; place in freezer; freeze until firm, 3 to 6 hours. Using a fork, beat 2 to 3 times while freezing.
Store in a covered container.

Makes 6 to 8 servings.

Boysenberry Ice Cream

375 g (12 oz./2 cups) fresh or frozen boysenberries,
strawberries or other berries
2 tablespoons water
185 g (6 oz./¾ cup) sugar
4 egg yolks
250 ml (8 fl. oz./1 cup) milk
250 ml (8 fl. oz./1 cup) single (light) cream
Vanilla extract to taste
Rich Brandy Sauce, page 118, if desired

TO GARNISH:
Sugared Fruit and Leaves, page 114, if desired

In a food processor/blender, process berries, 60 g (2 oz./¼ cup) sugar and water to a smooth purée. If desired, strain through a nylon strainer to remove seeds.

In a stainless steel bowl or top of a double boiler beat the remaining sugar and egg yolks until thick and creamy.

In a small saucepan, scald milk. Pour over eggs.

Place bowl or top of double boiler over a pan of gently simmering water. Stir slowly and continually 10 minutes. Remove from heat. Add cream and vanilla; cool.

Pour custard and berry juice into ice cream canister. Freeze in ice cream maker according to manufacturer's directions.

FREEZER METHOD: Mix custard and berry juice. Pour mixture into several ice trays; cover; place in freezer; freeze until firm, 3 to 6 hours. Using a fork, beat 2 to 3 times while freezing.

Store in a covered container. Serve with Rich Brandy Sauce and a cookie, if desired. Garnish with Sugared Fruit and Leaves, if desired.

Makes 6 servings

VARIATION:
Boysenberry Ripple: Prepare custard and fruit purée as in above recipe. Just before ice cream freezes add 125 ml (4 fl. oz./½ cup) of fruit purée. Stir just enough to give the ice cream a rippled effect. Serve remaining fruit purée as an accompanying sauce.

Avocado Ice Cream

Avocado pear enthusiasts enjoy this favoured fruit in any form. Serve avocado ice cream accompanied by a strong lime-flavoured liqueur. The combination is magical.

3 well-ripened avocado pears, halved, stoned
Juice of 1½ large lemons or limes
105 g (3½ oz./½ cup) sugar
600 ml (1 pint/2½ cups) single (light) cream

Scrape flesh from avocado shells. In a food processor/blender, process avocado, lemon or lime juice and sugar until smooth. Do not overprocess.

Pour avocado purée and cream into ice cream container. Freeze in ice cream maker according to manufacturer's directions.

FREEZER METHOD: Stir cream into avocado purée. Pour into several undivided ice trays; cover; place in freezer; freeze until firm, 3 to 6 hours. Using a fork, beat twice while freezing.

Store in a covered container.

Makes 6 to 8 servings.

VARIATION:
Place avocado shells in freezer while ice cream is prepared.

To serve, fill shells with ice cream, rounding top. Decorate with slices of lime or lemon and a mint leaf.

— *Ginger and Chocolate Soufflé* —

3 egg yolks
105 g (3½ oz./½ cup) sugar
250 ml (8 fl. oz./1 cup) milk
2 tablespoons cocoa or unsweetened carob powder
315 ml (10 fl. oz./1¼ cups) single (light) cream
90 g (3 oz./½ cup) crystallized ginger

TO GARNISH:
Chocolate Leaves, page 112, if desired
Candied Peel, page 115, if desired

In a stainless steel bowl or top of a double saucepan, whisk egg yolks and sugar until thick and creamy.

In a small saucepan, mix milk and cocoa or carob powder; scald. Pour over egg mixture; whisk thoroughly.

Place bowl or top of double saucepan over a pan of simmering water. Stir slowly and continually 10 minutes or until custard slightly thickens. Remove from heat; cool. Stir in cream if using ice cream maker.

In a food processor/blender, process ginger to a thick paste.

Pour custard into ice cream container. Freeze in ice cream maker according to manufacturer's directions. Add prepared ginger paste just before ice cream firmly freezes.

FREEZER METHOD: Stir ginger paste into custard. In a small bowl, lightly whisk cream. Fold into custard mixture. Pour mixture into several undivided ice trays; cover; place in freezer; freeze until firm, 3 to 6 hours. Using a fork, beat twice while freezing.

Store in a covered container.

Garnish with Chocolate Leaves and Candied Peel, if desired.

Makes 6 servings.

Chestnut Soufflé

105 g (3½ oz./½ cup) sugar
60 ml (2 fl. oz./¼ cup) water
6 egg whites
250 ml (8 fl. oz./1 cup) whipping cream
220 g (7oz./1 cup) sweetened chestnut purée/cream

To Garnish:
Chopped nuts, if desired
Whipped cream, if desired
Melted Chocolate, if desired

In a small thick saucepan, heat sugar and water gently, moving saucepan around carefully until sugar is dissolved. Do not stir. Cook over medium heat until mixture reaches hard ball stage 120C (250F).

In a medium bowl, whisk egg whites until voluminous but not stiff. Drizzle sugar syrup over egg whites in a slow, steady stream, whisking continually.

In a large bowl, whip cream with chestnut purée/cream until smooth and thick. Add egg whites; beat lightly.

Pour mixture into several undivided ice trays; cover; place in freezer; freeze until firm, 3 to 6 hours. Using a fork, beat once while freezing.

Store in a covered container.

Garnish with chopped nuts, whipped cream and melted chocolate, if desired.

Makes 8 servings.

— Pear and Benedictine Soufflé —

8 well-ripened pears, peeled, cored, halved
105 g (3½ oz./½ cup) sugar
3 egg yolks
3 egg whites
Small pinch of salt
125 ml (4 fl. oz./½ cup) whipping cream
1½ tablespoons Benedictine

To Garnish:
Pear slices, if desired
Mint leaves, if desired
Citrus strips, page 115, if desired

In a medium saucepan, cover pears with water. Cook over low heat; tightly covered, until tender.

In a food processor/blender, process pears and cooking liquid to a smooth purée.

In a stainless steel bowl or top of a double saucepan, whisk sugar and egg yolks. Add pear purée.

Place bowl or top of double saucepan over a pan of simmering water. Whisk custard 12 minutes until thick.

Remove from heat. Place bowl or top of double saucepan in a bowl of ice. Whisk until cool.

Whisk egg whites and salt to soft peaks. Fold into pear custard. In a small bowl, whip cream and Benedictine. Fold into custard mixture. Pour prepared mixture into several undivided ice trays; cover; freeze 2 hours before serving.

Garnish with pear slices, mint leaves and citrus strips, if desired.

Makes 4 to 6 servings.

VARIATION:
Spoon ice cream into individual freezer-proof dessert dishes; freeze. Dip slices of pear into salted water or lemon juice. Top with slices of pear and Sugared Leaves, page 114.

Mango Cream

2 large, well-ripened mangoes, halved lengthwise, stoned
2 tablespoons lime or lemon juice
60 ml (2 fl. oz./¼ cup) sugar syrup, page 64, or 2
tablepoons sugar
250 ml (8 fl. oz./1 cup) whipping cream

To Garnish:
Slices of melon or mango, if desired
Flaked almonds, if desired

Carefully scoop out mango flesh. Cover shells with cling film; refrigerate.

Chop mango flesh. In a food processor/blender, process mango with lime or lemon juice and sugar syrup or sugar until smooth and thick.

Pour mango purée and cream into ice cream container. Freeze in ice cream maker according to manufacturer's directions.

FREEZER METHOD: Pour mango purée into several undivided ice trays; cover; place in freezer; freeze to a slush. In a bowl, whip cream to soft peaks. Remove mango ice from freezer. Fold cream into mango ice. Return to trays. Recover; return to freezer. When almost firm, beat with a fork, or process in food processor/blender.

Store in a covered container.

Before serving, refrigerate 20 minutes to soften.

Garnish with slices of melon or mango and flaked almonds, if desired.

Makes 4 to 6 servings.

VARIATION:
Spoon ice cream into mango shells; cover; freeze. Garnish with flaked almonds, if desired.

—— *Coconut Banana Cream* ——

3 egg yolks
105 g (3½ oz./1½ cup) sugar
1 383 g (13½ fl. oz.) can coconut cream
Vanilla essence to taste
2 well-ripened bananas, mashed
375 ml (12 fl. oz./1½ cups) single (light) cream

In a stainless steel or heatproof glass bowl set over a pan of simmering water, whisk egg yolks, sugar and coconut cream 10 minutes or until thick and creamy. Do not overheat.

Remove from heat. Whisk until cool. Stir in vanilla, bananas and cream; mix thoroughly.

Pour into several undivided ice trays; cover; place in freezer; freeze until firm, 3 to 6 hours. Using a fork, beat every ½ hour.

Store in a covered container.

Before serving refrigerate 20 minutes to soften.

Makes 6 servings.

VARIATIONS:
Fill small ice cream moulds or a large bombe mould with Coconut Banana Cream. Add Rum and Raisin Ice Cream, page 25, when firm. Freeze, unmould on dessert plates. Garnish with desiccated coconut.

Fill pancakes with Coconut Banana Cream. Serve with fruit and toasted strips of almonds.

Black Cherry Cream

1 (383 g/13½ oz.) can stoned black cherries in syrup
250 ml (8 fl. oz./1 cup) whipping cream
2 tablespoons cherry brandy

To Garnish:
Melted chocolate, if desired
Maraschino cherries, if desired

In a food processor/blender, process cherries and syrup until smooth. Pour into an undivided tray; cover; place in freezer; freeze to a slush.

In a small bowl, whip cream to soft peaks. Fold in cherry brandy. Remove cherry ice from freezer. Fold cream into cherry ice; cover; refreeze.

When almost firm, beat with a fork, or process in food processor/blender. Freeze until firm.

Store in a covered container.

Before serving, refrigerate 20 minutes to soften.

Garnish with melted chocolate and a cherry, if desired.

Makes 4 servings.

VARIATION:
In tall parfait glasses, layer scoops of Black Cherry Cream with black cherries in syrup. Add whipped cream; top with Praline, page 110, or toasted flaked almonds.

Papaya Cream

900 g (2 lb.) fresh ripe papaya, peeled, seeded, cubed
125 ml (4 fl. oz./½ cup) sugar syrup, page 64
375 ml (12 fl. oz./1½ cups) single (light) cream

TO GARNISH:
Fresh fruit, if desired

In a food processor/blender, process papaya and sugar syrup to a purée.

Pour fruit purée and cream into an ice cream container. Freeze in ice cream maker according to manufacturer's directions.

FREEZER METHOD: Pour fruit purée into several undivided ice trays; cover; place in freezer; freeze to a slush. Remove from freezer. In a food processor/blender, process slush until smooth. Mix in cream. Pour mixture into ice trays, recover; freeze until firm.

Store in covered container.

Garnish with fruit, if desired.

Makes 6 servings.

Strawberry Cream

1 383 g (13½ oz.) can strawberries in heavy syrup
Juice of ½ lemon
375 ml (12 fl. oz./1½ cups) whipping cream
Syrup from can of strawberries, if desired

TO GARNISH:
Fresh strawberries, if desired

In a food processor/blender, process strawberries, half of syrup and lemon juice to a smooth purée.

In a small bowl, whip cream to soft peaks. Fold in strawberry purée. Pour into ice cream container. Freeze in ice cream maker according to manufacturer's directions.

FREEZER METHOD: Pour mixture into several undivided ice trays; cover; place in freezer; freeze until firm, 3 to 6 hours. Using a fork, beat 2 to 3 times while freezing.

Store in a covered container.

Serve over syrup from a can of strawberries, if desired.

Garnish with strawberries, if desired.

Makes 4 to 6 servings.

—— Macadamia Nut Parfait ——

8 egg whites
220 g (7 oz./1 cup) sugar
60 ml (2 fl. oz./¹/₄ cup) water
500 ml (16 fl. oz./2 cups) whipping cream
Vanilla essence to taste
125 g (4 oz./³/₄ cups) lightly toasted macadamia nuts,
hazelnuts, or pistachio nuts, chopped
Chocolate Cups, page 113, if desired

TO GARNISH:
Maraschino cherries dipped in melted chocolate, if desired

In a stainless steel or heatproof glass bowl beat egg whites until smooth and light, but not stiff.

In a small saucepan, heat sugar and water gently until sugar is dissolved; cook, without stirring, to hard ball stage 120C (250F).

Drizzle syrup in a thin stream into eggs, beating continuously until mixture is thick and smooth.

Pour cream, egg mixture and vanilla into ice cream container. Freeze in ice cream maker according to manufacturer's directions. Fold in nuts just before ice cream firmly freezes.

FREEZER METHOD: In a small bowl, lightly whip cream. Stir cream, vanilla and nuts into egg mixture. Pour mixture into several undivided ice trays; cover; place in freezer; freeze until firm, 3 to 6 hours. Using a fork, beat once while freezing.

Store in covered container.

Serve in Chocolate Cups, if desired.

Garnish with maraschino cherries dipped in melted chocolate, if desired.

Makes 6 to 8 servings.

VARIATIONS:
Plantation Parfait: In tall parfait glasses, spoon diced fresh tropical fruit (mango, papaya, pineapple and passionfruit). Add 2 scoops of Macadamia Nut Parfait ice cream. Add more tropical fruit. Cover top with whipped cream and Kiwi Fruit Purée, page 121, or Passionfruit Sauce, page 120. Decorate with a pineapple leaf.

Coffee Parfait

185 ml (6 fl. oz./³/4 cup) milk
1½ tablespoons instant coffee powder
8 egg yolks
330 g (10½ oz./1½ cups) sugar
125 ml (4 fl. oz./½ cup) water
950 ml (32 fl. oz./4 cups) whipping cream
Pinch of salt

To Garnish:
Chocolate Cups, page 113, if desired
Fresh strawberries, dipped in melted chocolate, if desired
Sweetened chocolate powder or grated chocolate, if desired

In a small saucepan, scald milk. Add coffee; cool.

In a stainless steel or heatproof glass bowl, whisk egg yolks until thick and creamy.

In a small saucepan, cook sugar and water over low heat, without stirring, to hard ball stage 120C (250F).

Pour caramel in a thin stream over egg yolks, whisking continuously. Beat until light and voluminous. Add coffee mixture.

In a medium bowl, whip cream and salt to soft peaks. Fold lightly into custard. Pour into several undivided ice trays; cover; place in freezer; freeze until firm, 3 to 6 hours. Using a fork, stir 3 to 4 times while freezing.

Store in a covered container.

Serve in Chocolate Cups with a strawberry dipped in melted chocolate, if desired. Dust with sweetened chocolate powder or grated chocolate, if desired.

Makes 8 servings.

VARIATION:

Coffee Parfait: In tall parfait glasses, spoon Coffee Parfait when ice cream is partly frozen; cover; freeze until firm. Prepare Spun Sugar, page 108, or Caramel Cages, page 109. Before serving, place on top of ice cream.

Ginger Parfait

250 ml (8 fl. oz./1 cup) milk
50 g (4 oz./¼ cup) sugar
85 g (3 oz./½ cup) chopped ginger preserved in syrup
2 eggs
375 ml (12 fl. oz./1½ cups) whipping cream
Biscuit, if desired

In a small saucepan, scald milk. Stir in sugar and ginger with syrup. Cover and remove from heat. Let sit 20 minutes.

In a stainless steel or heatproof glass bowl set over a pan of simmering water, whisk eggs until mixture is thick and creamy. Add milk mixture, beat 10 minutes. Remove from heat; Place bowl in a bowl of ice; whisk until cool.

Pour custard and cream into ice cream container. Freeze in ice cream maker according to manufacturer's directions.

FREEZER METHOD: In a small bowl, whip cream to soft peaks, fold into custard. Pour into several undivided ice trays; cover; place in freezer; freeze until firm, 3 to 6 hours.

Store in a covered container.

Serve with a biscuit.

Makes 6 servings.

VARIATION:
Serve Ginger Parfait with drained lychees, a Tuille, page 105, or ice cream wafer and preserved ginger syrup.

Raspberry Parfait

125 g (4 oz./²/₃ cup) fresh raspberries
220 g (7 oz./1 cup) sugar
60 ml (2 fl. oz./¼ cup) water
6 egg yolks
500 ml (16 fl.oz/2 cups) whipping cream

TO GARNISH:
Fresh raspberries, if desired
Mint leaves, if desired

In a food processor/blender, process raspberries to a smooth purée. If desired, strain through a fine nylon sieve to remove seeds.

In a small thick saucepan cook sugar and water over low heat until sugar is dissolved. Cook to hard ball stage 120C (250F).

In a stainless steel or heatproof glass bowl, whisk egg yolks. Drizzle sugar syrup over eggs in a thin stream, whisking continuously until mixture is thick and smooth. Continue whisking until cool.

Pour egg mixture, cream and raspberry purée into ice cream container. Freeze in ice cream maker according to manufacturer's directions.

FREEZER METHOD: In a small bowl, whip cream to soft peaks. Fold cream and raspberry purée into egg mixture. Pour mixture into several undivided ice trays; cover; place in freezer; freeze until firm, 3 to 6 hours. Using a fork, beat once while freezing.

Store in a covered container.

Garnish with raspberries and mint leaves, if desired.

Makes 6 servings.

Rhubarb Parfait

Humble rhubarb takes on a new importance in this subtly tart and delicate pink ice cream.

500 g (1 lb.) fresh young rhubarb, sliced
250 ml (8 fl. oz./1 cup) water
40 g (13 oz./1¾ cups) sugar
1 tablespoon water
5 egg yolks
500 ml (16 fl.oz./2 cups) whipping cream

TO GARNISH:
Poached rhubarb, if desired
Mint leaves or edible leaves, if desired

In a medium saucepan, cover rhubarb with water. Add 125 g (4 oz./½ cup) sugar. Cook, covered, over low heat 20 minutes or until very tender. Drain liquid from rhubarb; set aside. In a food processor/blender, process rhubarb to a smooth purée.

Taste rhubarb for sweetness. If very sweet, do not use all of remaining sugar. In a small saucepan, combine desired remaining sugar, water and reserved liquid from rhubarb. Cook over low heat without stirring to hard ball stage 120C (250F).

In a stainless steel or heatproof glass bowl, beat egg yolks until thick and creamy. Drizzle sugar syrup in a thin stream over eggs, beating continuously until mixture is light and fluffy.

Mix in rhubarb purée. In a medium bowl whip cream. Fold into rhubarb mixture; cover. Pour into several undivided ice trays; place in freezer; freeze until firm, 3 to 6 hours. Using a fork, beat 2 to 3 times while freezing.

Serve with poached rhubarb, if desired.

Garnish with mint leaves or edible leaves, if desired.

Makes 6 servings.

Maple Walnut Parfait

6 egg whites
1 egg yolk
105 g (3½ oz./½ cup) sugar
1 tablespoon water
60 ml (2 fl. oz./¼ cup) maple syrup
250 ml (8 fl.oz/1 cup) whipping cream
60-125 g (2 to 4 oz./½ to 1 cup) chopped walnuts or
pecans

In a stainless steel or heatproof glass bowl, whisk egg whites and yolk until thick and creamy.

In a small thick saucepan, cook sugar and water over low heat to hard ball stage 120C (250F).

Pour syrup over eggs in a thin stream, beating continually until thick and light. Stir in maple syrup. Pour maple mixture and cream into ice cream container. Freeze in ice cream maker according to manufacturer's directions. Fold in nuts just before parfait firmly freezes.

FREEZER METHOD: In a small bowl, whip cream to soft peaks. Fold cream and nuts into maple mixture. Pour mixture into several undivided ice trays; cover; place in freezer; freeze until firm, 3 to 6 hours.

Store in a covered container.

Makes 6 servings.

VARIATION:
Maple and Walnut Mould: Do not add chopped walnuts to maple mixture. After beating, pour ½ maple mixture into a wet ice cream mould or a large ice tray; cover; freeze. Add ½ nuts to remaining maple mixture. Pour over frozen parfait. Cover. Freeze until firm. Unmould; slice to serve. Place slices on maple syrup; serve with a biscuit, garnish with remaining nuts.

Frozen Strawberry Yogurt

Plain yogurt can be used to make tasty and nutritious ice creams, and is an ideal dessert alternative in diets where kilojoule (calorie) intake is carefully monitored.

1 383 g (13½ oz.) can strawberries in light syrup
500 ml (16 fl. oz./2 cups) plain yogurt
125 ml (4 fl. oz./½ cup) whipping cream

To Garnish:
*Fresh strawberries, if desired
Marshmallows, if desired*

In a food processor/blender, process strawberries and syrup to a smooth purée. Add yogurt and cream; blend until smooth and thoroughly mixed.

Pour into ice cream container. Freeze in ice cream maker according to manufacturer's directions.

FREEZER METHOD: Pour into several undivided ice trays; place in freezer.

Cover; freeze until firm, 3 to 6 hours. Using a fork, beat twice while freezing.

Store in covered container.

Before serving, refrigerate 20 minutes to soften.

Garnish with a strawberry and a marshmallow, if desired.

Makes 6 to 8 servings.

Healthy Peach Ice Cream

*This ice cream is made with skimmed milk powder instead of cream and can
be adapted for the diet-conscious by using skim milk.*

*1 875 g (1¾ lb.) can peaches in natural juice
2 egg yolks
2 tablespoons sugar or substitute sweetener to taste
375 ml (12 fl. oz./1½ cups) milk or skimmed milk
45 g (1½ oz./½ cup) skimmed milk powder
Fresh fruit, if desired*

*To Garnish:
Mint leaves, if desired*

In a food processor/blender, process peaches and syrup to a smooth
purée.

In top of a double saucepan, whisk egg yolks with sugar until
thick and creamy.

In a small saucepan, scald milk. Stir in skimmed milk powder until
dissolved. Place top of double saucepan over pan of simmering water.
Pour milk over eggs, stir slowly and continually 10 minutes or until
custard slightly thickens. Remove from heat; pour custard and peach
purée into ice cream container. Freeze in ice cream maker according to
manufacturer's directions.

FREEZER METHOD: Stir peach purée into custard. Pour into several
undivided ice trays; cover; place in freezer; freeze until firm, 3 to 6
hours. Using a fork, beat 2 to 3 times while freezing.

Garnish with mint leaves, if desired.

Store in a covered container.

Before serving refrigerate 30 minutes to soften. Serve with fresh
fruit, if desired.

Makes 6 servings.

—— Carob Honey Frozen Yogurt ——

Homemade frozen yogurt tastes better and fresher than the store-bought kind, and you can vary the sweetness according to your taste and kilojoule (calorie) requirements.

500 ml (16 fl. oz./2 cups) plain yogurt
125 g (4 oz./¹/₃ cup) honey
45 g (1¹/₂ oz./¹/₃ cup) unsweetened carob powder
125 ml (4 fl. oz./¹/₂ cup) whipping cream, if desired
Fresh fruit, if desired

In a medium bowl, whip yogurt until smooth. Stir in honey and carob powder.

In a small bowl, whip cream, if desired. Stir into yogurt mixture.

Pour prepared mixture into several undivided ice trays; cover; place in freezer; freeze until firm, 3 to 6 hours. Using a fork, beat twice while freezing.

Store in a covered container.

Serve with fruit, if desired.

Makes 6 servings.

– *Apricot Soybean Milk Ice Cream* –

75 g (2½ oz./²/₃ cup) dry soybean milk powder
250 ml (8 fl. oz./2 cups) cold water
90 g (3 oz./½ cup) dried apricots
185 ml (6 fl. oz./¾ cup) water
250 g (8 oz./¾ cup) honey

To Garnish:
Crystallized apricots if desired
Strips of cucumber peel, if desired

In a small bowl, dissolve soybean milk powder in cold water; set aside. In a small saucepan, cook apricots in 60 ml (2 fl. oz./¼ cup) water or until tender. In a food processor/blender, process apricots and cooking liquid to a smooth purée. Mix in honey. Mix soybean milk with apricot purée.

Pour into ice cream container. Freeze in ice cream maker according to manufacturer's directions.

FREEZER METHOD: Pour prepared mixture into several undivided ice trays; cover; place in freezer; freeze until firm, 3 to 6 hours. Using a fork, beat 3 to 4 times while freezing.

Store in a covered container.

Before serving, refrigerate to soften.

Garnish with crystallized apricots and strips of cucumber peel, if desired.

Makes 6 to 8 servings.

Sorbets

The exciting revolution in cooking techniques that characterised *nouvelle cuisine* also heralded changes in dining habits. Gone were the heavy sauces and ponderous consumption of excessive quantities of food, to be replaced by a refreshing lightness of taste and considerably smaller servings. More variety, less volume, real food flavours were the goals.

Sorbets, served both as a stimulating, palate cleansing, between-course highlight, and as a dessert, often with an assortment of fresh fruits, were rediscovered. The pure fruit flavours, cooling and subtle, perfectly complemented and rounded the innovative new menus.

A good sorbet is an enchantment of smooth, icy texture, tart sweetness and delicate fruit flavour. One might think sorbets would be difficult to make at home. At least, one would expect less than perfect results without a sorbetière (a special sorbet storage container) or an ice cream sorbet maker.

But, surprisingly, sorbets are quite simply made and a food processor/blender will give excellent results.

The rules are few: the mixture must have a certain level of sugar in order to freeze properly. Too much and the sorbet will remain wet and syrupy and will separate after a time; too little and the liquids will form large ice crystals giving a grainy texture, spoiling the flavour.

The sugar content of the sorbet mixture (fruit juice or purée, sugar and water) is checked on a sugar gauge (saccharometer). As the average household does not have this equipment, I have given measurements for volume of fruit to sugar/sugar syrup which should give good results.

Fresh fruit sorbets made with fruit juice or purée, sugar syrup and perhaps lemon or lime juice to counter oversweetness, are the best. They should be made to be served the same day in order to enjoy their full fruit flavour and aroma. Storing does not improve sorbets. They begin to form ice crystals as well as lose much of their taste.

Alcohol-flavoured sorbets similarly do not keep well and should be consumed as soon as possible after being made. They take longer to freeze than fruit sorbets.

Whisked egg whites are often added to sorbets after they have been partially frozen – to a stage which is referred to as a 'slush' (see next page). The reason for this addition, which perhaps surprisingly does not impart an eggy taste, is to bind the ice and give a firmer and smoother consistency to the sorbet. However, egg whites are unnecessary when the sorbet is churned in an ice cream maker.

HOW TO MAKE A FRUIT SORBET

Very juicy fruits such as citrus, berries, melons and pineapple make the best sorbets. The juice can be extracted, or whole fruit puréed in a food processor/blender and used strained or unstrained according to preference.

A sugar syrup is added along with a quantity of water if the fruit juice/purée is particularly thick or strongly flavoured. An uncarbonated mineral water, instead of plain water, gives a little extra zing to a sorbet.

Freezing diminishes both taste and sweetness, so when judging quantities of sugar to fruit when making your own recipes, tend towards a slightly oversweet, well-flavoured mixture. When frozen, the sorbet should be just right.

The mixture should be poured into ice trays or any container suitable for freezing, covered with cling film or foil and frozen to a 'slush'. At this state the sorbet will have begun to firm up on the bottom and sides of the container. It will be thickish and icy in the centre, although still semi-liquid.

It is then beaten briskly in a food processor/blender, or with a hand-held electric mixer, before returning to the freezer. The beating incorporates air and emulsifies the mixture, breaking up ice crystals and making it smoother in texture and lighter in colour.

Very delicate fruits such as melons and lychees should not be overbeaten or processed as this destroys their subtle flavour.

USING AN ICE CREAM MAKER

A sorbet can be completed in an ice cream maker and ready to serve within 40 minutes if you like a firm sorbet, or straight from the churn in 20-25 minutes if you enjoy it soft textured.

Pour the mixture into a cooled churn/ice cream maker and churn until velvety smooth and thick. It will harden with extra freezing and should be transferred to a covered container in the freezer, if your ice cream maker does not have an automatic freezer control.

Leftover sorbet which has lost much of its original appeal can be reprocessed or blended to restore its texture and rejuvenated by the addition of a liqueur. Or it can be served with a fruit purée sauce.

SERVING SORBETS

Sorbets served between courses should be of the tart or savoury kind, such as grapefruit or other citrus, champagne or cucumber. Serve only small portions, with minimal decoration – perhaps a single mint leaf or a tiny sprig of fresh herbs. The aim is to refresh the palate, not add a course to the menu.

With dessert sorbets your imagination can be given full rein. Try shaping the sorbet into ovals between two tablespoons – it's a traditional way of presenting sorbet. Arrange a platter of several sorbets with an array of fresh fruits or flowers. Pile ovals or scoops of sorbet into champagne flutes or tall parfait glasses. Add a flourish of fruit cubes or a bunch of sugar-frosted grapes. Or you can freeze layers of different sorbets in an ice cream mould and serve in slices.

— SHERBETS, GELATI AND GRANITAS —

Sherbets fall somewhere between sorbets, feather-light fruity ices, and full rich creamy custard-based ice creams. The Italian gelato is perhaps a perfect example, strongly flavoured, yet icy and milky textured.

Sherbets are economical ices to make requiring milk, sugar and a good flavouring agent rather than expensive mixtures of cream and eggs.

Sherbets are easy to make, simply mixed, frozen and beaten once or twice. They are firmer textured and melt quicker once served. But they are quite delicious, and best served with a combination of flavours – strawberry, chocolate and vanilla are a classic trio and require no embellishment except perhaps a single fresh strawberry or flurry of chocolate flakes.

Granitas are water-based ices which are frozen and left unbeaten/unprocessed. The mixture forms hard ice crystals, an essential part of a granitas character. Granitas, too, rely on strong flavours. Lemon and coffee granitas are classics that are enjoyed around the world.

Sugar Syrup

Sugar syrup is quickly made. When cooled, syrup can be refrigerated in a covered glass or plastic container for 2 to 3 weeks.
This amount is sufficient for at least 4 recipes.

1 kg (2 lb.) caster sugar
950 ml (32 fl. oz./4 cups) water

In a large saucepan bring sugar and water to a gentle boil. Reduce heat until bubbles break surface. Simmer 10 minutes. Remove from heat; cool before using or storing.

Lemon Sorbet

Finely grated rind of 1 lemon
250 ml (8 fl. oz./1 cup) water
185 g (6 oz./¾ cup) sugar
250 ml (8 fl. oz./1 cup) lemon juice (about 6 lemons)
310 ml (10 fl. oz./1¼ cups) uncarbonated mineral water
1 egg white, whisked

In a saucepan, simmer rind, water and sugar 10 minutes; cool.

In a medium bowl, mix sugar syrup, lemon juice and mineral water. Pour into ice cream container. Freeze in ice cream maker according to manufacturer's directions. Egg white can be added before sorbet freezes or omitted, if desired.

FREEZER METHOD: Pour prepared mixture into several undivided ice trays or a cake tin; cover; place in freezer; freeze to a slush. In a food processor/blender, process semi-frozen sorbet and egg white 1 minute until smooth and light. Return to tray. Recover; freeze until firm.

Makes 6 servings.

Orange Sorbet

Grated rind of 1 orange
375 g (12 fl. oz./1½ cups) water
220 g (7 oz./1 cup) sugar
500 ml (16 fl. oz./2 cups) orange juice (about 4 large
oranges)
250 ml (8 fl. oz./1 cup) uncarbonated mineral water

TO GARNISH:
Orange slices, if desired
Mint leaves, if desired

In a medium saucepan, simmer rind with water and sugar 20 minutes; cool. Strain sugar syrup. Set rind aside.

In a medium bowl, combine sugar syrup, orange juice and mineral water. Pour into ice cream container. Freeze in ice cream maker according to manufacturer's directions. Fold in orange rind just before sorbet firmly freezes.

Garnish with orange slices and mint leaves, if desired.

FREEZER METHOD: Pour prepared mixture into several undivided ice trays. Place in freezer; freeze to a slush.

In a food processor/blender, process semi-frozen sorbet until smooth. Stir in orange rind. Return to trays; cover; freeze until firm.

Makes 6 servings.

VARIATION:
Orange Parfait: Peel several juicy oranges, cutting through flesh. Using a sharp knife, remove each segment separately without pith. Arrange orange segments in dessert dishes. Top with several scoops of Orange Sorbet. Cover with Grand Marnier Sauce, page 116. Add whipped cream.

Lime Sorbet

Limes are quite expensive, so in this recipe lemon juice is added to fresh lime juice to make it more economical, but without loss of flavour. If preparing fresh sugar syrup, add finely grated rind of lime to syrup. Cook for 10 minutes. Drain; reserve rind to use as a garnish.

60 ml (2 fl. oz./¹⁄₃ cup) lime juice (about 2-3 limes)
60 ml (2 fl. oz./¹⁄₄ cup) lemon juice (about 2 fresh lemons)
500 ml (16 fl. oz./2 cups) sugar syrup, page 64
310 ml (10 fl. oz./1¹⁄₄ cups) water or uncarbonated mineral water
1 egg white, whisked

To Garnish:
Lime slices and Citrus Strips, page 115, if desired
Mint leaves or edible leaves, if desired

In a medium mixing bowl, mix lime and lemon juice, sugar syrup and mineral water. Omit egg white. Pour into ice cream container. Freeze in ice cream maker according to manufacturer's directions. Transfer to a freezer container; cover; freeze until firm.

FREEZER METHOD: Pour prepared mixture into several undivided ice trays; cover with foil; place in freezer; freeze to a slush. In a medium bowl, beat semi-frozen sorbet and egg white until light and smooth. Return to trays; recover; freeze until firm.

Garnish with lime slices, Citrus Strips and mint leaves or edible leaves, if desired.

Makes 6 servings.

Strawberry Sorbet

560 g (1¼ lb/4 cups) fresh ripe strawberries, hulled, wiped
500 ml (16 fl. oz./2 cups) sugar syrup, page 64
Juice of ½ orange
Juice of ½ lemon

To Garnish:
Fresh strawberries, if desired
Mint leaves or edible leaves, if desired

In a food processor/blender, process strawberries and ½ of sugar syrup to a smooth purée. Mix in remaining syrup and orange and lemon juice. Pour into several undivided ice trays; cover; place in freezer; freeze to a slush. Return to food processor/blender. Process until light and smooth. Return to trays; re-cover; freeze until firm.

Garnish with strawberries and mint leaves or edible leaves, if desired.

Makes 6 to 8 servings.

VARIATIONS:
Strawberry Marsala Sorbet: add 75 ml (2½ fl. oz./⅓ cup) marsala. Substitute lemon juice for orange juice.

Strawberry Orange Sorbet: add 375 ml (12 fl. oz./1½ cups) orange juice and juice of ½ lemon or lime.

Add 250 ml (8 fl. oz./1 cup) of single cream when processing last time.

Kiwi Fruit Sorbet

Kiwi fruit, also known as a Chinese gooseberry, has in recent times upstaged strawberries as a garnish for sweet and savoury dishes alike. Its vivid green hue and delicate, flower-like placement of tiny black seeds in the centre of each slice, makes an appealing food decoration.

6 ripe kiwi fruit, peeled, trimmed, cubed
410 ml (13 fl. oz./1²/₃ cups) sugar syrup, page 64
185 ml (6 fl. oz./³/₄ cup) uncarbonated mineral water
Slices of kiwi fruit, if desired

TO GARNISH:
Lime slices, if desired

In a food processor/blender, process kiwi fruit to purée.

Mix in sugar syrup and mineral water. Pour into ice cream container. Freeze in ice cream maker according to manufacturer's directions.

FREEZER METHOD: Pour prepared mixture into several undivided ice trays; cover; place in freezer; freeze to a slush.

Return to food processor/blender. Process until smooth and lighter in colour. Return to trays; cover; freeze until firm.

Serve with slices of kiwi fruit, if desired.

Garnish with lime slices, if desired.

Makes 6 to 8 servings.

Pineapple Sorbet

1 large pineapple, peeled, cored, cubed
Juice of 1 lime or lemon
75 g (2½ oz./⅓ cup) sugar

In a food processor/blender, process pineapple, lime or lemon juice and sugar to a smooth purée. Pour into ice cream container. Freeze in ice cream maker according to manufacturer's directions.

FREEZER METHOD: Pour prepared mixture into several undivided ice trays; cover; place in freezer; freeze 1 hour. Return to food processor/blender. Process until smooth and velvety. Return to trays, recover; freeze until firm.

Makes 6 servings.

VARIATIONS:
Pineapple Crème de Menthe Sorbet: Add 2 tablespoons of white crème de menthe to semi-frozen sorbet partway through churning or after processing last time.

Fruit Salad Sorbet: Stir diced pineapple, passionfruit pulp, banana, mango, papaya and lime juice into Pineapple Sorbet just before sorbet freezes.

Cut pineapple lengthwise, cutting through leaves. Scoop flesh from shells. Freeze shells until sorbet is almost firm. Fill pineapple shells with sorbet. Cover with foil. Freeze until firm. Serve in shell. Garnish with mint leaves and Citrus Strips, page 115.
    Or fill frozen pineapple shells with balls of pineapple or other tropical fruit sorbets, garnish with desiccated coconut or toasted almonds and embellish with cocktail umbrellas or fresh flowers.

— *Honeydew and Ginger Sorbet* —

1.125 kg (2½ lb) honeydew melon, peeled, cubed
1½ teaspoons finely chopped fresh ginger
Juice of 1 lemon
500 ml (16 fl. oz./2 cups) sugar syrup, page 64
1 egg white, whisked
Slices of melon, if desired

TO GARNISH:
Mint leaves, if desired

In a food processor/blender, process melon to a purée. Mix in ginger, lemon juice and sugar syrup. Omit egg white.

Pour into ice cream container. Freeze in ice cream maker according to manufacturer's directions until sorbet holds shape. Transfer to a freezer container; cover. Freeze until firm.

FREEZER METHOD: Pour prepared mixture into several undivided ice trays; cover; place in freezer; freeze to a slush. Return to food processor/blender. Process semi-frozen sorbet and egg white until smooth. Return to trays; recover; freeze until firm.

Serve in slices of melon, if desired.

Garnish with mint leaves, if desired.

Makes 8 to 10 servings.

VARIATION:
Line small custard cups with cling film. Fill with sorbet when partially frozen. Pack firmly; smooth top. Remove by pulling cling film. Invert onto a plate; remove cling film. Surround with thin slices of melon, overlapped in a rose petal formation.

Raspberry Sorbet

315 g (10 oz./2 cups) fresh or frozen raspberries
250 ml (8 fl. oz./1 cup) sugar syrup, page 64
1 egg white, whisked

TO GARNISH:
Mint leaves or edible leaves, if desired

In a food processor/blender, process berries and ½ cup sugar syrup to a smooth purée. If desired, strain through a fine sieve. Omit egg white.

Pour raspberry purée and remaining sugar syrup into ice cream container. Freeze in ice cream maker according to manufacturer's directions. Transfer to a freezer container; cover. Freeze until firm.

FREEZER METHOD: Mix raspberry purée and remaining sugar syrup. Pour into an undivided ice tray; cover; place in freezer; freeze to a thick slush.

In a food processor/blender, process semi-frozen sorbet and egg white until light and smooth. Return to tray; recover; freeze until firm.

Garnish with mint leaves or edible leaves, if desired.

Makes 4 to 6 servings.

VARIATION:
Raspberry Roses: Place a large single scoop or sorbet in centre of a dessert plate. Using a tablespoon, press down around edge, gently pressing petal shapes outwards. Work towards centre, using smaller spoons. Surround with Sugared Leaves, page 114.

Melon Sorbet

1 medium ripe cantaloupe melon, halved, seeded
125 ml (4 fl. oz./¹/₂ cup) sugar syrup, page 64
Slices of melon, if desired

TO GARNISH:
Mint leaves, if desired

Using a melon baller or spoon, remove melon flesh. In a food processor/blender, process melon and sugar syrup to a smooth purée. Do not over process.

Pour into ice cream container. Freeze in ice cream maker according to manufacturer's directions until sorbet holds shape. Transfer sorbet to a freezer container; cover; place in freezer; freeze until firm.

FREEZER METHOD: Pour prepared mixture into several undivided ice trays; place in freezer; freeze to a slush. Return to food processor/blender. Process briefly until smooth and fluffy. Return to trays; cover; freeze until firm.

Makes 6 servings.

VARIATIONS:
Freeze melon shells. Fill shells with Sorbet when sorbet is firmly frozen. Cover with foil. Freeze until firm. Cut in slices, cutting through shell.

Serve with slices of melon, if desired. Garnish with mint leaves, if desired.

Melon and Passionfruit Sorbet: Add 2 to 3 tablespoons of passionfruit pulp when preparing sorbet. In tall parfait glasses, arrange balls of sorbet. Top with Passionfruit Sauce, page 120.

Grape Sorbet

750 ml (24 fl. oz./3 cups) red or white grape juice

To Garnish:
Sugared Grapes, page 114, if desired
Grape leaves, if desired

Pour juice into ice cream container. Freeze in ice cream maker according to manufacturer's directions.

FREEZER METHOD: Pour juice into several undivided ice trays. Place in freezer; freeze until almost firm. In a food processor/blender, process semi-frozen sorbet until smooth. Return to trays; freeze until firm.

To serve, spoon in tall parfait or champagne flutes. Garnish rim of glass with Sugared Grapes and a grape leaf, if desired.

Makes 6 servings.

VARIATION:
Fruit Juice Sorbets: Substitute commercial blend of fruit juice for grape juice, or concentrated fruit juices. Add water or uncarbonated mineral water and sugar syrup to taste, page 64.

Papaya Sorbet

1 1.25 kg (2½ lb.) fresh ripe papaya, peeled, seeded, cubed
125 ml (4 fl. oz./½ cup) sugar syrup, page 64
Juice of 1 large lime
Fresh fruit, if desired

To Garnish:
Mint leaves, if desired

In a food processor/blender, process papaya, sugar syrup and lime juice to a smooth, thick purée. Pour into ice cream container. Freeze in ice cream maker according to manufacturer's directions.

FREEZER METHOD: Pour prepared mixture into several undivided ice trays. Place in freezer; freeze to a slush. Return to food processor/blender. Process until smooth. Return to trays; cover; freeze until firm.
Serve with fresh fruit, if desired.
Garnish with mint leaves, if desired.

Makes 6 servings.

VARIATION:
Form oval shapes by filling a tablespoon with sorbet and pressing another spoon over top. Serve with sugared lime slices.
Or team with Guava Sorbet, page 78, and fresh fruit.

Watermelon Sorbet

5 to 6 kg (10 to 12 lb.) watermelon, cubed
375 ml (12 fl. oz./1½ cups) sugar syrup, page 64
Juice of 1 lime or lemon
2 egg whites, whipped

TO GARNISH:
Watermelon slices, if desired
Mint leaves, if desired

In a food processor/blender, process melon to a thin liquid. Measure 1L (32 fl. oz./4 cups) juice.

Mix melon juice, sugar syrup and lime or lemon juice, omit egg whites. Pour into ice cream container. Freeze according to manufacturer's directions until almost firm. Transfer to a freezer container. Freeze until firm.

Freezer method. Pour prepared mixture into several individual ice trays. Cover with a foil. Place in freezer; freeze to a thick slush. Return ½ of semi-frozen to food processor/blender. Process with 1 egg white until smooth. Return to trays. Cover; freeze until firm. Repeat with remaining mixture and egg white.

Garnish with watermelon slices and mint leaves, if desired.

Makes 8 to 10 servings

VARIATION:
Tropical Sorbet Gâteau: Line a cake pan with a removable bottom with foil.

Freeze layers of watermelon, pineapple, passionfruit, mango and kiwi fruit sorbets; one layer at a time.

To serve, cut gâteau into wedges. Serve with a kiwi fruit purée or fresh fruit salad.

Lychee and Ginger Sorbet
1 510 g (18 oz.) can lychees in heavy syrup
250 ml (8 fl. oz./1 cup) water
90 g (3 oz./1/2 cup) drained ginger preserved in syrup

In a food processor/blender, process lychees and syrup until reasonably smooth. Set aside. Process water and ginger to a similar consistency. Mix lychees and ginger mixtures.

Pour into ice cream container. Freeze in ice cream maker according to manufacturer's directions until just firm. Transfer to a freezer container. Cover; freeze until firm.

FREEZER METHOD: Pour prepared mixture into several undivided ice trays. Place in freezer; freeze to a slush. Return to food processor/blender. Process until smooth. Return to trays; cover; freeze until firm.

Makes 4 to 6 servings.

VARIATIONS:
Drain another can of lychees thoroughly. Using a small melon baller, scoop out balls of sorbet. Insert one into each lychee. Freeze until lychees are firm. Serve on cocktail sticks with coffee.

Spoon scoops of Lychee and Ginger Sorbet into glass dessert dishes. Top with finely chopped preserved ginger and a dash of the ginger syrup. Garnish with mint leaves or edible leaves, if desired.

Guava Sorbet

Tropical guavas are an unusual fruit. Their bright pink colour and sweet, sharp taste produce an interesting sorbet.

250 g (8 oz.) guavas (about 6), peeled
125 ml (4 fl. oz./½ cup) water
185 ml (6 fl. oz./¾ cup) sugar syrup, page 64

To Garnish:
Fresh lime peel, if desired

In a food processor/blender, process guavas and water to a purée. Strain through a fine nylon sieve, pressing with a wooden spoon. Discard seeds.

Pour fruit purée and sugar syrup into ice cream container. Freeze in ice cream maker according to manufacturer's directions.

FREEZER METHOD: Mix fruit purée and sugar syrup. Pour into several undivided ice trays; cover; place in freezer; freeze to a thick slush. Return to food processor/blender. Process until smooth. Return to trays; recover; freeze until firm.

Garnish with lime peel, if desired.

Makes 4 servings.

Passionfruit Sorbet

250 ml (8 fl. oz./1 cup) passionfruit pulp (8 to 10 ripe
passionfruit)
125 g (4 oz.½ cup) sugar syrup, page 64
250 ml (8 fl. oz./1 cup) uncarbonated mineral water
Fresh fruit, if desired

Pour passionfruit pulp, sugar syrup and mineral water into ice cream
canister. Freeze in ice cream maker according to manufacturer's
directions until almost firm. Transfer to a freezer container; cover.
Place in freezer; freeze until firm.

FREEZER METHOD: In a medium bowl, mix passionfruit pulp,
sugar syrup and mineral water. Pour into several undivided ice trays;
place in freezer; freeze to a slush. Using a fork, beat vigorously.
Cover; freeze until firm.
Serve with fresh fruit, if desired.

Makes 6 to 8 servings.

VARIATIONS:
In tall parfait glasses, place scoops of Passionfruit, Pineapple and
Papaya or Mango Sorbets. To garnish, thread cubes of tropical fruit
onto cocktail sticks or short bamboo skewers.

Sandwich a layer of Passionfruit Sorbet between two layers of
Chocolate Gelato, page 87, or Chocolate Ice Cream, page 16. Freeze
until firm. To serve, slice in wedges and cover with Passionfruit
Sauce, page 120.

Champagne Sorbet

315 ml (10 fl. oz./1¼ cups) sugar syrup, page 64
½ bottle pink or white champagne or dry sparkling wine
Juice of ½ lemon
½ egg white, whisked

To Garnish:
Mint leaves, if desired

In a medium bowl, mix syrup, champagne and lemon juice. Pour into ice cream container. Freeze in ice cream maker according to manufacturer's directions until just firm. Transfer to a freezer container. Stir in egg white; cover, place in freezer; freeze until firm.

FREEZER METHOD: Pour prepared mixture into several undivided ice trays; cover; place in freezer; freeze to a slush. Return to food processor/blender. Process semi-frozen sorbet and egg white until light and smooth. Return to trays. Recover; freeze until firm. Serve within 2 to 3 hours.
  Spoon sorbet into iced champagne glasses.
  Garnish with mint leaves and grapes, if desired.

Makes 6 servings.

Port and Lemon Sorbet

250 ml (8 fl.oz./1 cup) fresh lemon juice (4 to 6
lemons)
500 ml (16 fl. oz./2 cups) water
105 g (3½ oz./½ cup) sugar
185 ml (6 fl. oz./¾ cup) ruby port
1 egg white, whisked

To Garnish:
Lemon slices, if desired
Mint leaves, if desired

In a medium bowl, mix lemon juice, water, sugar and port. Stir until sugar dissolves. Add egg white only if following freezer method.

Pour in ice cream container. Freeze in ice cream maker according to manufacturer's directions.

FREEZER METHOD: Pour prepared mixture into several undivided ice trays; cover; place in freezer; freeze to a thick slush. In a food processor/blender, process semi-frozen sorbet and egg white until light and smooth. Return to trays. Recover; freeze until firm. Serve within 2 to 3 hours.

Pile sorbet in chilled champagne flutes.

Garnish with a lemon slice and a mint leaf, if desired.

Makes 6 to 8 servings.

Crème de Menthe and Orange Sorbet

250 ml (8 fl. oz./1 cup) orange juice, strained
250 ml (8 fl. oz./1 cup) water
125 ml (4 fl. oz./1/2 cup) sugar syrup, page 64
60 ml (2 fl. oz./1/4 cup) green crème de menthe

To Garnish:
Leaves, if desired
Citrus Strips, page 115, if desired
Pieces of orange, if desired

In a medium bowl, mix all ingredients. Pour into ice cream container. Freeze in ice cream maker according to manufacturer's directions.

FREEZER METHOD: Pour prepared mixture into several undivided ice trays; cover; place in freezer; freeze to a slush.

In a food processor/blender, process semi-frozen sorbet until light and smooth. Return to trays; recover; freeze until firm.

Garnish with mint leaves, Citrus Strips and pieces of orange, if desired.

Makes 6 servings.

— *Grapefruit and Vodka Sorbet* —

375 ml (12 fl. oz./1½ cups) fresh grapefruit juice (about 3 grapefruit)
250 ml (8 fl. oz./1 cup) water
250 ml (8 fl. oz./1 cup) sugar syrup, page 64
60 ml (2 fl.oz./¼ cup) vodka

To Garnish:
Sugared Flowers, page 114, if desired
Citrus Strips, page 115, if desired

Pour grapefruit juice, water and sugar syrup into ice cream container. Freeze in ice cream maker according to manufacturer's directions until almost firm. Add vodka. Churn until thick. Transfer to a freezer container; cover; freezer until firm.

FREEZER METHOD: In a medium bowl, mix grapefruit juice, water and sugar syrup. Pour into several undivided ice trays; cover; place in freezer; freeze to a thick slush.

In a food processor/blender, process semi-frozen sorbet until light and smooth. Add vodka. Return to trays; recover; freeze until firm.

Garnish with Sugared Flowers and Citrus Strips, if desired.

Makes 6 to 8 servings.

— *Sherbet of Pears in Red Wine* —

8 ripe pears, peeled, cored, halved lengthwise
250 ml (8 fl. oz./1 cup) red wine
250 ml (8 fl. oz./1 cup) water
1 small cinnamon stick
105 g (3½ oz./½ cup) sugar
250 ml (8 fl. oz./1 cup) single (light) cream
8 Tuilles, page 105, if desired

To Garnish:
Fresh grapes, if desired
Mint leaves, if desired

In a large saucepan, cover pears with wine and water. Add cinnamon stick; sprinkle sugar evenly over pears.

Simmer, covered, 18 minutes or until pears are very tender. Remove cinnamon stick; cool.

In a food processor/blender, process pears and liquid to a purée. Pour pear purée and cream into ice cream container. Freeze in ice cream maker according to manufacturer's directions.

FREEZER METHOD: In a bowl blend pear purée and cream. Pour into several undivided ice trays; cover; place in freezer; freeze to a thick slush. Return to food processor/blender. Process semi-frozen sorbet and cream until light and well blended. Return to trays; recover; freeze until firm.

Store in a covered container.

Serve with Tuilles, if desired.

Garnish with grapes and mint leaves, if desired.

Makes 8 servings.

VARIATION:
Shape firm sherbet into pear shapes. Add a Sugared Mint Leaf, page 114, to each. Serve with a piped rosette of whipped cream flavoured with a pear liqueur or Cognac.

Pear and Pernod Ice

Pernod makes a perfect partner for fresh pears.

625 g (1¼ lb.) ripe pears (4 to 5 pears),
peeled, cored, cubed
125 ml (4 fl. oz./½ cup) sugar syrup, page 64
125ml (4 fl. oz./½ cup) water
Juice of 1 lemon
2½ tablespoons Pernod

To Garnish:
3 pears, halved, cored, if desired
Mint leaves, if desired

In a food processor/blender, process pears and sugar syrup until smooth. Add water and lemon juice.

Pour into ice cream container. Freeze in ice cream maker according to manufacturer's directions until thick. Add Pernod. Freeze until smooth. Transfer to a freezer container; cover; place in freezer; freeze until firm.

FREEZER METHOD: Pour prepared mixture into several undivided ice trays. Place in freezer; freeze to a slush. Return to food processor/blender. Process frozen sorbet and Pernod until light and smooth. Return to trays; cover. Freeze until firm.

Serve within 4 to 6 hours.

Serve in ½ pear, if desired.

Garnish with mint leaves, if desired.

Makes 6 servings.

VARIATION:

Orange Pear Ice: Substitute orange or mandarin liqueur for Pernod. Serve with Mandarin Sauce, page 120, or Grand Marnier Sauce, page 116.

- *Ginger Mandarin Liqueur Sorbet* -

1 tablespoon finely grated fresh ginger
1 (315 g/10 oz.) can mandarins
60 ml (2fl. oz./¹/4 cup) sugar syrup, page 64
60 ml (2fl. oz./¹/4 cup) mandarin liqueur or Curaçao
Melon balls, if desired

In a food processor/blender, process ginger, mandarins and liquid and sugar syrup to a smooth purée. If using ice cream maker, stir in mandarin liqueur or Curaçao.

Pour into ice cream canister. Freeze in ice cream maker according to manufacturer's directions.

FREEZER METHOD: Pour mandarin purée into several undivided ice trays; cover, place in freezer; freeze to a slush.

Return to food processor/blender. Process until smooth. Add mandarin liqueur or Curaçao. Return to trays; recover; freeze until firm.

Serve with melon balls, if desired.

Makes 6 servings.

Chocolate Gelato

750 ml (24 fl. oz./3 cups) milk
220 g (7 oz./1 cup) sugar
125 g (4 oz.) plain (dark) chocolate, coarsely grated
Biscuits, if desired

TO GARNISH:
Chocolate Caraque, page 113
Sugared Flowers, page 114, if desired

In a medium saucepan, cook milk and sugar over low heat 10 minutes. Stir occasionally to dissolve sugar.

Mix chocolate with hot milk. Cook until chocolate completely dissolves.

Pour into ice cream container. Cool. Freeze in ice cream maker according to manufacturer's directions.

FREEZER METHOD: Pour prepared mixture into several ice trays; cool; cover; place in freezer; freeze until firm. Using a fork, beat every 30 minutes 3 to 4 times while freezing.

Serve with a biscuit, if desired.

Garnish with Chocolate Caraque and Sugared Flowers, if desired.

Makes 6 to 8 servings.

Vanilla Gelato

750 ml (24 fl. oz./3 cups) milk
1 vanilla pod
185 g (6 oz./³⁄₄ cup) sugar

To Garnish:
Sugared Fruit, page 114, if desired
Mint leaves, if desired

In a saucepan, bring milk and vanilla pod to boiling point. Remove from heat; cool. When pod is soft, insert point of a small, sharp knife near top. Cut in ½. Scrape small seeds into milk. Stir in sugar until dissolved; cool.

Strain milk through a fine nylon sieve into ice cream container. Freeze in ice cream maker according to manufacturer's directions.

FREEZER METHOD: Strain milk into several undivided ice trays; cover; place in freezer; freeze until firm. Using a fork, beat every 30 minutes, during freezing.

Garnish with Sugared Fruit and Mint Leaves, if desired.

Makes 6 servings.

Lemon Granita

Unlike sorbets which have a smooth soft texture, granitas are frozen flavoured ices.

250 ml (8 fl. oz./1 cup) lemon juice (4 to 6 lemons)
500 ml (16 fl. oz./2 cups) water
105 g (3½ oz./½ cup) sugar

To Garnish:
Mint leaves, if desired

In a medium bowl, mix juice, water and sugar. Stir until sugar completely dissolves. Pour into several undivided ice trays; cover; place in freezer; freeze until firm.

Before serving, refrigerate to soften enough to scrape into dishes. Garnish with mint leaves, if desired.

Makes 6 servings.

VARIATION:
Substitute lime or grapefruit juice, or a mixture of citrus juices for lemon juice.

Coffee Granita

500 ml (16 fl. oz./2 cups) water
15 g (½ oz./¼ cup) instant coffee powder
185 ml (6 fl. oz./¾ cup) sugar syrup, page 64
Biscuits, if desired
Chocolate Cups, page 113, if desired

TO GARNISH:
Mint leaves, if desired
Melted chocolate, if desired
Strawberry slices, if desired

In a small saucepan, bring 250 ml (8 fl. oz./1 cup) water and coffee powder to a boil, stirring until coffee powder dissolves. Cool. Mix in sugar syrup and remaining water. Pour into several undivided ice trays; cover; place in freezer; freeze until firm.

Serve in Chocolate Cups with biscuits if desired.

Garnish with a mint leaf, a sliced strawberry or melted chocolate, if desired.

Makes 4 to 6 servings.

Japanese Green Tea Ice

60 ml (2fl. oz./¼ cup) boiling water
1¼ tablespoons Japanese green tea leaves
2 egg whites
155 g (5 oz./1 cup) icing sugar
1 egg yolk
375 ml (12 fl. oz./1½ cups) whipping cream
Green food colouring, if desired

In a small bowl, pour boiling water over tea leaves. Steep until cold. Strain tea liquid.

In a small bowl, beat egg whites to soft peaks. Add sugar, 1 tablespoon at a time. Beat in egg yolk, then cooled tea liquid.

In a small bowl, beat cream to soft peaks. Fold into ice. If desired, add 2 to 3 drops colouring.

Pour into several undivided ice trays; cover; place in freezer, freeze until firm.

Makes 6 servings.

Peppermint Tea Sorbet

500 ml (16 fl. oz./2 cups) water
15 g (½ oz./¼ cup) peppermint tea leaves
125ml (4 fl. oz./½ cup) sugar syrup, page 64

To Garnish:
Lemon slices, if desired
Mint leaves, if desired

In a small saucepan, boil water; add tea leaves. Cover and steep 3 hours. Strain through a fine nylon sieve.

Mix tea liquid and sugar syrup. Pour into an ice cream container. Freeze in ice cream maker according to manufacturer's directions.

FREEZER METHOD: Pour prepared mixture into several undivided ice trays. Place in freezer; freeze to a slush.

In a food processor/blender process semi-frozen sorbet 1 minute or until light. Return to trays; cover; freeze until firm.

Garnish with slices of lemon and mint leaves, if desired.

Makes 6 servings.

— Lime and Basil Sorbet —

Highlight a flavour-packed Mexican meal or rich Indian curry courses with Lime and Basil Sorbet.

250 ml (8 fl. oz./1 cup) lime juice (5 to 6 limes), strained
250 ml (8 fl. oz./1 cup) water
250 ml (8 fl. oz./1 cup) sugar syrup, page 64
12 fresh basil leaves, finely chopped

To Garnish:
Basil leaves or edible leaves, if desired
Slices of melon, if desired

Pour lime juice, water and sugar syrup into ice cream container. Add basil leaves. Freeze in ice cream maker according to manufacturer's directions.

FREEZER METHOD: In a medium bowl, mix lime juice, water and sugar syrup. Stir in basil leaves.

Pour into several undivided ice trays; cover. Place in freezer; freeze to a slush.

In a food processor/blender, process semi-frozen sorbet until smooth. Return to trays; cover; freeze until firm.

Garnish with basil leaves or edible leaves and slices of melon, if desired.

Makes 6 to 8 servings.

— Minted Grapefruit Sorbet —

Grated rind of ½ grapefruit
125 g (4 oz./½ cup) sugar
375 ml (12 fl. oz./1½ cups) water
500 ml (16 fl. oz./2 cups) grapefruit juice (about 3
grapefruits)
1½ teaspoons chopped fresh mint

In a small saucepan, simmer rind with sugar and water 10 minutes.
Cool. Strain through a fine nylon sieve. Set rind aside. In a medium
bowl, mix strained sugar syrup, juice and mint.

Pour into ice cream container. Freeze in ice cream maker according
to manufacturer's directions until almost firm. Add rind. Freeze until
firm.

FREEZER METHOD: Pour prepared mixture into several undivided
ice trays; cover; place in freezer; freeze to a slush. In a food
process/blender, process until smooth and creamy. Return to trays;
recover; freeze until almost firm. Stir in rind. Freeze until firm.

Makes 6 servings.

VARIATION:
Cut grapefruit in ½. Scoop flesh from shells; place shells in freezer.
Fill shells with semi-frozen sorbet. Cover; freeze until firm.

Garnish with leaves.

Savoury Melon Sorbet

1 kg (2 lb.) cantaloupe melon, peeled, seeded, cubed
250 ml (8 fl. oz./1 cup) chicken stock (or 2 chicken stock
cubes dissolved in 250 ml (8 fl. oz./1 cup) water)
Juice of 1 lemon
125 ml (4 fl. oz./½ cup) single (light) cream
3 to 4 basil leaves, chopped
Dash of Tabasco
Salt and pepper to taste
Pieces of melon, if desired

To Garnish:
Sprig of rosemary, if desired

In a food processor/blender, process melon and chicken stock to a smooth purée. Mix in remaining ingredients, except melon.

Pour into ice cream container. Freeze in ice cream maker according to manufacturer's directions.

FREEZER METHOD: Pour prepared mixture into several undivided ice trays. Place in freezer; freeze until almost firm.

In a food processor/blender, process until smooth. Return to trays; cover; freeze until firm.

Serve on pieces of melon, if desired.

Garnish with sprigs of rosemary, if desired.

Makes 8 servings.

—— *Tomato and Basil Sorbet* ——

6 ripe tomatoes
Juice of 1 large lemon
75 ml (2½ fl. oz./⅓ cup) sugar syrup, page 64
3 chives, finely chopped
6 to 8 fresh basil leaves, finely chopped
185 ml (6 fl. oz./¾ cup) tomato juice
Salt and pepper to taste
Dash of Tabasco, if desired

To Garnish:
Cucumber slices, if desired
Sprigs of rosemary, if desired

Drop tomatoes in a large saucepan of boiling water 8 seconds. Remove with a slotted spoon. Peel, scraping off the soft flesh beneath skin. Cut tops from peeled tomatoes. Scoop out seeds; discard. In a food processor/blender, process tomato flesh, lemon juice, sugar syrup, chives and basil leaves until smooth. Strain through a nylon strainer, using a wooden spoon to force pulp through. Add tomato juice, salt, pepper and Tabasco, if desired, to tomato purée.

Pour into ice cream container. Freeze in ice cream maker according to manufacturer's directions. Transfer to a freezer container; cover; place in freezer; freeze until firm.

FREEZER METHOD: Pour into several undivided ice trays; cover; place in freezer; freeze to a slush.

Return to food processor/blender. Process semi-frozen sorbet until smooth. Return to trays; recover; freeze until firm.

Garnish with cucumber slices and sprigs of rosemary, if desired.

Makes 6 to 8 servings.

—— Cucumber and Mint Sorbet ——

1 teaspoon chicken stock powder
125ml (4 fl. oz./½ cup) hot water
125ml (4 fl. oz./½ cup) plain yoghurt
1 tablespoon chopped fresh mint
Small pinch freshly ground black pepper
2 large cucumbers, peeled, cored, finely grated
Salad vegetables, if desired

In a small bowl dissolve chicken bouillon granules in hot water. In a small bowl, beat yoghurt. Add mint and pepper.

Mix yoghurt and cucumber with chicken bouillon. Pour into an ice cream container. Freeze in ice cream maker according to manufacturer's directions until almost firm. Transfer to a freezer container; cover. Place in freezer; freeze until firm.

FREEZER METHOD: Pour prepared mixture into several undivided trays. Place in freezer; freeze to a slush. Beat vigorously; cover; freeze until firm.

Before serving, refrigerate 15 minutes. Serve with salad vegetables, if desired.

Makes 6 to 8 servings.

VARIATION:
Using a vegetable peeler or lemon squeezer, remove long strips of lemon rind. Place in a dish of ice water to crisp and curl; drain. To serve, arrange strips of rind around sorbet. Garnish with cucumber slices and mint leaves.

Serve as a first course with a small salad.

Ice Cream Cakes & Concoctions

Chocaholics Fantasy

1 scoop Chocolate Supreme Ice Cream, page 15
2 chopped walnuts
1 scoop White Chocolate Ice Cream, page 15, or French
Vanilla Ice Cream, page 12
3 tablespoons Hot Fudge Sauce, page 116, or 2 tablespoons
melted plain (dark) chocolate
1 scoop Chocolate Gelato, page 87
60 ml (2 fl.oz/¼ cup) whipping cream, whipped
2 walnut halves
Chocolate covered biscuit

In a tall parfait glass, assemble Chocolate Supreme Ice Cream. Top with ½ of chopped walnuts and White Chocolate Ice Cream or French Vanilla Ice Cream. Top with ½ of Hot Fudge Sauce or chocolate. Add Chocolate Gelato. Cover with remaining chopped walnuts.

Top Chocaholics Fantasy with whipped cream; drizzle remaining Hot Fudge Sauce or melted chocolate over whipped cream. Add walnut halves and biscuit.

Makes 1 serving

Coupe Marrons Glacés

6 tablespoons sweetened chestnut purée
125ml (4 fl. oz./½ cup) whipping cream
6 scoops French Vanilla Ice Cream, page 12
6 scoops Chestnut Soufflé, page 45
Whipped cream
6 walnut halves
Biscuits, if desired

In a small bowl, beat chestnut purée and cream. Divide between 6
coupe glasses. Top with scoops of Vanilla Ice Cream and Chestnut
Soufflé. Cover with whipped cream. Garnish with walnuts
    Serve with a biscuit, if desired.

Makes 6 servings.

— *Raspberry Gâteau Jacqueline* —

Raspberry Sorbet, page 72
French Vanilla Ice Cream, page 12
315 g (10 oz./2 cups) raspberries
Raspberry Parfait, page 55

To Garnish:
Raspberry Purée, page 121, if desired
Fresh raspberries, if desired
Edible leaves, if desired

Smoothly line a straight-sided loaf tin with foil. Allow enough overhang on sides to cover top.

Soften Raspberry Sorbet to be workable but still hold shape. Spread 1.25-cm (½-in) layer evenly on sides, ends and bottom of tin. Reserve enough to cover top. Freeze until firm.

Soften Vanilla Ice Cream. Lightly stir in raspberries. Do not crush. Spoon into a rectangular dish same length as tin. Cover with foil; freeze.

Freeze Raspberry Parfait in a similar dish.

Cut 2 pieces each of Vanilla Ice Cream and Raspberry Parfait, each long enough to fit into tin and large enough so 4 strips will half fill tin.

Press 1 strip of vanilla and 1 of raspberry into tin. Place remaining 2 on top, on opposite sides, to give gâteau a chequerboard effect. Freeze until firm. Soften remaining Raspberry Sorbet. Cover top of chequerboard. Press foil firmly into place. Return gâteau to freezer until ready to serve.

Garnish with Rasberry Purée, raspberries and leaves, if desired.

Makes 8 to 10 servings.

Cassata

Chocolate Gelato, page 87, softened
Vanilla Gelato, page 88, softened
1 tablespoon chopped glacé cherries
1 tablespoon chopped candied peel
1 tablespoon chopped raisins
1 tablespoon chopped pistachio nuts
2 tablespoons Curaçao or other orange liqueur

TO GARNISH:
Maraschino cherries, if desired

Smoothly line a straight-sided loaf tin with foil.

Spread a 1.2 cm (½-in) layer of Chocolate Gelato on sides, ends and bottom of pan, reserving enough to cover top. Freeze until hard.

In a medium bowl, mix Vanilla Gelato and remaining ingredients. Place in freezer.

When chocolate base is frozen, fill with Vanilla Gelato mixture. Cover lightly; freeze until firm. Cover top with remaining Chocolate Gelato; freeze again.

Serve sliced.

Garnish with cherries, if desired.

Makes 8 servings.

Bombe Tropicana

This is an ideal way to use up leftover ice creams, so no specific amounts are given. Make bombe as small or as large as needed. Vary ice creams according to preference.

French Vanilla Ice Cream, page 12, softened
Passionfruit Ice Cream, page 36, softened
Pineapple Ice Cream, page 40, softened
Egg whites
Caster sugar
Fruit salad, drained
Desiccated coconut

To Garnish:
Tropical flowers and leaves, if desired

In a round mould or container of a suitable size, spread a thick layer of vanilla ice cream. Layer should be curved from rim of container down sides and over bottom leaving a hollow in centre. Freeze firm.

Add a layer of Passionfruit Ice Cream, using above procedure, freeze again. Spread a layer of Pineapple Ice Cream.

Add fruit salad. Cover; freeze until ice cream is extremely firm. Do not remove ice cream from freezer until ready to apply and bake meringue.

Preheat oven to 230C (450F).

In a small bowl, whisk egg whites. Three whites and 105 g (3½ oz./½ cup) sugar is sufficient for a bombe large enough to serve 6 to 8 people. Whisk in sugar 1 tablespoon at a time. Continue whisking until meringue is stiff and glossy.

Unmould frozen bombe on a heatproof plate. Cover with fruit salad. Quickly spread meringue over fruit and ice cream, covering completely.

Using a knife, make swirls and peaks in meringue. Sprinkle desiccated coconut on bombe. Bake in preheated oven until meringue is browned, 4 to 5 minutes.

Garnish with flowers and leaves, if desired.

Serve immediately.

—— *Chocolate Praline Gâteau* ——

*This is a good way to dress up a plain chocolate cake, turning it into an
exquisite dessert. Either fresh or frozen chocolate cake may be used. Serve
with or without whipped cream.*

*1 round chocolate cake
Praline Ice Cream, page 17, softened
125 g (4 oz.) plain (dark) chocolate, melted*

*To Garnish:
Chocolate Leaves, page 112, if desired*

Cut cake in 3 even layers. Reassemble; freeze until very cold.

Spread Praline Ice Cream thickly between slices of cake.
Reassemble cake. Wrap in cling film or foil. Freeze until very firm.

Spoon chocolate into a small paper piping bag. Snip off end. Pipe a
lacy pattern over top and sides of cake.

Garnish with Chocolate Leaves, if desired.

Makes 8 to 10 servings.

— *Chocolate Ice Cream Truffles* —

Chocolate Ice Cream, page 16, solidly frozen
60 g (2 oz.) plain (dark) chocolate, chopped
2 tablespoons cocoa powder
24 Meringue Baskets, page 107, if desired

In a food processor/blender, process chocolate and cocoa to fine crumbs. Pour into a shallow bowl. Using a spoon, scoop walnut-sized balls of ice cream.

Insert a thin wooden skewer into ice cream ball. Roll ice cream in chocolate. Remove stick. Insert cocktail stick. Repeat procedure for remaining ice cream balls. Freeze until firm. Serve in Meringue Baskets, if desired.

Makes 24 truffles.

Cases, Decorations & Sauces

Tuilles

105 g (3½ oz./½ cup) sugar
75 g (2½ oz./½ cup) plain flour
Vanilla essence to taste
1½ large egg whites
2½ tablespoons ground almonds

Preheat oven to 200C (400F). Grease a baking sheet. In a medium bowl, mix all ingredients thoroughly. Using a spatula dipped in cold water, spread mixture thinly in small round shapes on prepared baking sheet. Bake in a preheated oven 6 minutes or until golden brown around edge.

Remove with spatula. Form into tuille shape by gently and quickly folding biscuit over handle of a wooden spoon. Remove from handle.

Store in an airtight container up to 3 weeks.

VARIATION:
Dip double edge of Tuilles into melted chocolate, and if desired, into chopped toasted almonds.

Makes 36 Tuilles.

Crisp Ice Cream Cases

60 g (2 oz./¼ cup) butter or margarine, softened
105 g (3½ oz./½ cup) caster sugar
2 egg whites
Vanilla essence to taste
75 g (2½ oz./½ cup) plain flour

Preheat oven to 180C (350F). Line 2 to 3 baking sheets with greaseproof paper.

In a medium bowl, cream butter or margarine and sugar until smooth. Whisk in egg whites lightly; add vanilla.
Using a spatula, gently fold in flour.

Cut a cardboard stencil 15 cm (6-inches) in diameter. Hold in position on prepared baking sheets. Draw lightly around stencil. Spread mixture and thinly inside circle. Bake in preheated oven 6-7 minutes or until golden brown.

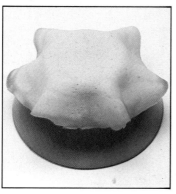

Remove from baking sheet by sliding a spatula underneath while still hot. Shape by pressing into small lightly oiled brioche moulds or hanging over inverted lightly oiled cups while still hot.
When cool, remove from moulds with tip of a knife. Store in an airtight container.

Makes 12 cups.

Meringues

6 egg whites
325 g (10½ oz./1½ cups) caster sugar
Small pinch of salt

Preheat oven to 170C (325F). Line a baking sheet with silicone paper.

In a stainless steel or copper bowl whisk egg whites and salt to stiff peaks.

Whisk in 220 g (7 oz./1 cup) of sugar. Whisk 1 minute; fold in remaining sugar.

Spoon meringue on prepared baking sheet in 18 rounds 5 cm (2-inches) in diameter and peaked in centre.

Bake in preheated oven 1 hour or until firm and dry. Remove from oven before meringues begin to colour.

Makes 18 meringues.

VARIATION:

Meringue Baskets: To make small baskets spread meringue in 12 thick, round shapes 7.5 cm (3-inches) in diameter on prepared baking sheet. Spoon remaining meringue into a piping bag fitted with a star nozzle. Pipe 2 to 3 rows around edge to build rim. Bake as directed above.

To make 2 large meringue baskets increase size of base to 22.5 cm (9-inches) diameter and form deeper sides.

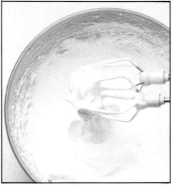

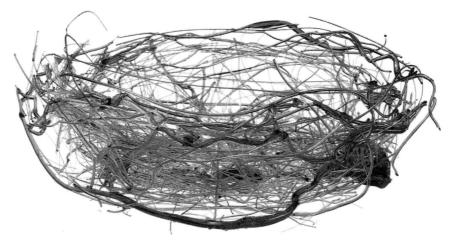

Spun Sugar (Angel's Hair)

A fine web of golden spun sugar makes an entrancing decoration for an ice cream or sorbet. Decorate with violets or chocolate-dipped flaked almonds. It can be prepared several hours in advance and is fun to do.

220 g (7 oz./1 cup) sugar
185 ml (6 fl. oz./¾ cup) water or golden syrup

In a medium saucepan, simmer sugar and water, without stirring, to 150C (300F), or until a drop of toffee solidifies immediately when dropped in cool water.

Cover floor of work area with newspaper. Suspend the handle of a wooden spoon over the newspaper-covered area.

Using 2 large forks and, working quickly, dip forks lightly into syrup. Wave over spoon handle so syrup is thrown in very fine threads and hangs over handle.

When syrup has been spun, gather up and stand in a cool place until needed. Do not allow spun sugar to become moist.

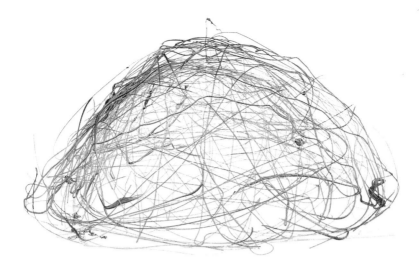

Caramel Cages

220 g (7 oz./1 cup) sugar
75 g (2½ oz./⅓ cup) water
Pinch of cream of tartar

In a small saucepan combine all ingredients. Bring to boil.

Reduce heat. Simmer gently, without stirring. To remove crystals, brush sides of pan with a wet pastry brush.

Cook to 170C (340F).

Remove from heat. Let stand 5 to 6 minutes or until syrup darkens.

Cover back of a small ladle with foil; grease.

Hold ladle over pan. Using a spoon to drizzle caramel syrup over ladle, form a web. Form a solid edge of toffee around rim of ladle to maintain shape of cage when removed from ladle.

Working quickly, lift completed cage from ladle. Set carefully to retain rounded shape.

Re-cover ladle; repeat process. Caramel should remain soft enough to complete 6 cages. If not, gently reheat for 10 seconds. Do not allow to boil.

Caramel cages can be made 4 hours in advance.

Makes 6 cages.

Praline

220 g (7 oz./1 cup) sugar
2 tablespoons water
90 g (3 oz./¾ cup) toasted whole almonds, skins intact

Grease a baking sheet. In a medium saucepan, simmer sugar and water without stirring, to hard crack stage 150C (300F) or until a drop of syrup solidifies immediately when dropped in cool water.

Add almonds. Pour on prepared baking sheet. Let set until hard. Break into pieces. In a food processor/blender, process until fine. Store in a covered container in a cool place.

Makes 310 g (10 oz./2 cups).

Toffeed Strawberries

12 to 18 ripe, plump strawberries, with stems
220 g (7 oz./1 cup) sugar
60 ml (2fl. oz./¼ cup) water
Large pinch of cream of tartar

Grease a plate. In a medium saucepan, stir sugar and water until sugar is moist. Cook over medium heat 5 minutes. Add cream of tartar. Cook to hard crack stage 150C (300F) or until a drop of toffee solidifies immediately when dropped in cool water.

Remove from heat. Holding a strawberry by the stem or by a fork, draw it through toffee, tilting pan so toffee will cover strawberry. As strawberry is lifted, twist to release from toffee.

Set on greased plate to harden. Repeat procedure for remaining strawberries. Serve within 30 minutes.

Makes 12 to 18 strawberries.

- *Chocolate Ice Cream Decorations* -

Chocolate goes beautifully with ice cream. Its crunch and strong flavour highlights smooth texture and subtle flavours to perfection. Chocolate can be shaped into leaves, boxes or cups, and batons. Or, it can be used as a complete covering, either by being preformed or poured over ice cream.

Chocolate Leaves: Dip underside of leaves into melted plain (dark) or white chocolate. Or using a small brush, paint underside of leaves with melted chocolate. Place on a baking sheet, chocolate-covered side upwards. Refrigerate until firm. Gently separate leaves from chocolate.

Chocolate Curls: Chocolate block should be soft enough to scrape, but firm enough for the curls to hold their shape. Using a sharp vegetable peeler, peel off curls of chocolate. Use individually or roll curls together to make shapes. Larger rolls (chocolate batons) can be used as a garnish for parfaits.

Chocolate Cups: Using a small brush, spread melted plain (dark) chocolate evenly over inside of small foil dishes. Cool. Refrigerate until firm. Before using peel foil from chocolate.

Other Decorations: Spread melted plain (dark) chocolate thinly on parchment paper. When chocolate begins to firm cut in small square boxes, square, round or rectangular tops for ice cream gâteaux, or shape into circles while chocolate is soft enough to mould. Let set. Carefully peel paper from chocolate.

Chocolate Caraque: Pour melted chocolate to a ¼-cm (⅛-in) thickness on back of baking (biscuit) sheet. Let set. Holding cutting edge of a sharp knife at a 45 degree angle push knife away from you, separating chocolate from baking (biscuit) sheet. Chocolate will roll and form long scrolls as knife edge moves along under it.

– *Sugared Fruit, Flowers & Leaves* –

Sugared fruits give an elegant and summery look to ice creams and sorbets.

Whole fruits with stems, flowers or leaves, rinsed, dried
1 egg white
Caster sugar

In a small bowl, using a fork, lightly beat egg white until slightly frothy.

Holding by stem or inserting a fork into fruit, dip fruit, flowers or leaves in egg white. Or use a small brush to coat all surfaces evenly. Brush off excess.

Coat evenly with sugar. Dry on a sugared surface 30 minutes or until sugar forms a crisp, dry coating.

Strawberry Fans

Select plump, well-coloured straw-berries with stems attached. Using a small, sharp knife, hold stem and make several cuts from just below stem end of fruit to point. Pinch base gently between thumb and forefinger to fan out slices.

Citrus Strips and Candied Peel

Using a lemon zester, remove long strips of peel from oranges, lemons or grapefruit. Let stand in bowl of ice water to curl. Use to decorate citrus-flavoured sorbets or ice cream.

To make candied peel, in a small saucepan, simmer citrus strips in a mixture of equal parts of sugar and water until peel looks transparent and syrup begins to colour. Remove strips; dry on a wire rack. Or, serve with syrup.

Crystallized Citrus Fruit

3 oranges, limes or lemons, thinly sliced
220 g (7 oz./1 cup) sugar
375 ml (12 fl. oz./1½ cups) water
Caster sugar

In a medium saucepan, boil sugar and water 3 to 4 minutes. Add fruit. Reduce heat. Simmer 45 minutes or until skin turns transparent. Cool fruit on a wire rack set over a baking sheet. Coat thickly with caster sugar. Dry on rack 48 hours. Refrigerate in an airtight container.

Hot Fudge Sauce

185 g (6 oz.) plain (dark) chocolate, chopped
125ml (4 fl. oz./1/2 cup) water
2 tablespoons butter or margarine
1 tablespoon single (light) cream

In a small saucepan cook chocolate and water over low heat until chocolate melts, whisk in butter or margarine and cream. Serve hot.

Makes 375 ml (12 fl. oz./1½ cups).

Grand Marnier Sauce

Superb over Chocolate Gelato, page 87, Chocolate Ice Cream, page 16, or Vanilla Ice Cream, page 14.

220 g (7 oz./1 cup) sugar
125ml (4 fl. oz./1/2 cup) Grand Marnier
Rind of 1 orange, finely grated
Juice of 1 orange

In a small heavy saucepan, heat sugar over low heat until dissolved. Add Grand Marnier, rind and orange juice. Simmer 5 minutes. Remove from heat; cool completely.

Refrigerate in a covered container up to 3 weeks.

Makes 375 ml (12 fl. oz./1½ cups).

Vanilla Cream Sauce

Serve Vanilla Cream Sauce with well-flavoured ice creams such as Chocolate, Raspberry or Coffee Praline. It combines well with Heavenly Honey Chocolate Sauce, page 119, and Fruit Purées, page 121.

2 egg yolks
50 g (1¾ oz./¼ cup) sugar
Vanilla essence to taste
375 ml (12 fl. oz./1½ cups) single (light) cream

In a bowl or top of a double boiler, beat egg yolks and sugar until thick and creamy.
In a small saucepan, scald cream. Pour over eggs; stir thoroughly. Add vanilla.

Place bowl or top of double saucepan over a pan of simmering water. Stir slowly and continually until mixture coats back of spoon and is consistency of cream.
Strain through a fine nylon sieve into a bowl. Cover with cling film. Press film on surface of sauce to prevent a skin forming. Chill.

Makes 500 ml (16 fl. oz./2 cups).

VARIATIONS:
Add liqueurs, cognac or rum to taste.

Chocolate Cream Sauce: Add 125 g (4oz.) melted plain (dark) chocolate to hot custard. Stir over low heat until completely blended.

Add chocolate to ½ of custard. Serve 2 sauces together.

Butterscotch Sauce

250 ml (8 fl. oz./1 cup) single (light) cream
185 g (6 oz./1/2 cup) golden syrup
90 g (3 oz./1/2 cup) soft brown sugar
2 tablespoons butter or margarine, chopped
Vanilla essence to taste
Small pinch of salt

In a small heavy saucepan, bring sugar, syrup and cream to a boil. Simmer over low heat 3 to 4 minutes. Add butter or margarine, vanilla and salt. Stir until butter or margarine melts and is completely blended.

Remove from heat; cool completely. Refrigerate in a covered container up to 3 weeks.

Makes 500 ml (16 fl. oz./2 cups).

Rich Brandy Sauce

105 g (3 1/2 oz./1/2 cup) sugar
125ml (4 fl. oz./1/2 cup) water
2 egg yolks
60 ml (2fl. oz./1/4 cup) cognac or brandy
60 ml (2fl. oz./1/4 cup) whipping cream, lightly whipped,
if desired

In a small saucepan, bring sugar and water to a boil. Reduce heat. Boil until syrup reaches soft ball stage 120C (250F).

In a small bowl, beat egg yolks until thick and creamy. Pour hot syrup over eggs, beating continually until sauce is thick and smooth. Add brandy; beat until cool.

If desired, fold cream into sauce before serving.

Makes 375 ml (12 fl. oz./1 1/2 cups).

- *Heavenly Honey Chocolate Sauce* -

250 ml (8 fl. oz./1 cup) single (light) cream
125 g (4 oz./⅓ cup) honey
90 g (3 fl. oz./¼ cup) golden syrup
(3 oz.) plain (dark) chocolate pieces
2 tablespoons crème de caçao, Drambuie or whisky

In a small thick saucepan, bring cream, honey and golden syrup to a boil. Reduce heat. Simmer 2 to 3 minutes. Add chocolate pieces. Simmer until chocolate melts. Stir occasionally.

Remove from heat. Add liqueur; cool completely.

Refrigerate in a covered container up to 3 weeks.

Makes 500 ml (16 fl. oz./2 cups).

Rum Sauce

105 g (3½ oz./½ cup) sugar
2 tablespoons water
185 ml (6 fl. oz./¾ cup) single (light) cream
60 ml (2 fl. oz./¼ cup) dark rum

In a small saucepan, cook sugar and water gently until sugar has dissolved then cook until syrup caramelizes and is golden brown.

Add cream. Stir over low heat until caramel dissolves completely.

Remove from heat; stir in rum. Serve hot or cold.

Refrigerate in a covered container up to 3 weeks.

Makes 375 ml (12 fl. oz./1½ cups).

Mandarin Sauce

4 mandarin oranges
105 g (3½ oz./½ cup) sugar
1½ teaspoons cornflour
2 to 3 tablespoons mandarin liqueur, if desired

Peel the mandarins and squeeze for juice. Scrape the rind of two mandarins with the back of a kitchen knife in order to remove all the white pith. Shred the rind very finely. Discard the remaining skin and pulp.

In a small saucepan, cover rind with cold water. Bring to a boil; boil 2 minutes. Drain; set rind aside.

Cook sugar in pan until a golden brown. In a small bowl, stir cornflour into juice. Pour over toffee. Add peel. Simmer, stirring until sauce slightly thickens and toffee dissolves. Add liqueur, if desired. Serve hot or cold.

Makes 375 ml (12 fl. oz./1½ cups).

Passionfruit Sauce

250 ml (8 fl. oz./1 cup) passionfruit pulp (about 10 passionfruit)
50 g (1¾ oz./¼ cup) sugar
185 ml (6 fl. oz./⅔ cup) water
1 tablespoon cornflour
2 tablespoons Curaçao, or other orange or mandarin liqueur

In a small saucepan, combine sugar, water and cornflour. Cook over low heat, stirring continually until mixture begins to thicken. Add passionfruit pulp. Boil gently 1 to 2 minutes, stirring continually.

Remove from heat. Cool slightly; add liqueur.

Makes 500 ml (16 fl. oz./2 cups).

Fruit Purées

Serve puréed fresh fruits as a sauce over fruit sorbets. Or, cover a flat dessert plate with purée; place ice cream in the centre.

Raspberries, boysenberries, strawberries, kiwi fruit mangoes or papayas peeled, seeded, chopped
Sugar Syrup, page 64
Lime or Lemon juice

In a food processor/blender, process fruit to a purée.

Add sugar syrup and lime or lemon juice to taste. Strain through a fine nylon strainer to remove seeds, if desired.

Iced Glasses

*Water, fruit juice or coloured water
Ice cream or sorbet*

Fill freezer-proof serving glasses with water, fruit juice or coloured water.

Freeze until ice has formed a good firm layer on inside of glass. Pour out liquid. Return glasses to freezer. Before serving, fill with ice cream or sorbet.

Ice Bowls and Rings

Frozen desserts can be extravagantly and elegantly presented in ice bowls or rings.

Cooled, boiled clear or coloured water
Small flowers and fresh fruit, if desired

In a large freezer-proof bowl, pour 1 to 2.5 cm (⅓ to 1-inch) water. Add fruits and flowers, if desired. Place in freezer until frozen. Remove from freezer.

Place smaller freezer-proof bowl inside larger one, firmly sitting on ice base. Add additional fruit and flowers, if desired. Place a weight in inner bowl.
Carefully pour water to rim of larger bowl.

Return to the freezer until water is solidly frozen.
Remove weight. Wipe inner bowl with a very hot cloth. When inner bowl releases, repeat with outer side of larger bowl. Return ice bowl to freezer until needed.

Serving Suggestions

A selection of sorbets: Raspberry (page 72), Passionfruit (page 79),
Strawberry (page 68) and Kiwi Fruit (page 69).

Roses (page 72) and Sherbet of Pears in Red Wine made into pear shapes
(page 84).

Coffee Parfait (page 53) served in a glass and in Chocolate Cups (page 113).

Banana Split made from French Vanilla Ice Cream (page 12), Neapolitan Strawberry Ice Cream (page 41), Heavenly Honey Chocolate Sauce (page 119), crushed nuts, banana, cherry, mint leaves and wafer.

Black Cherry Cream (page 49) and Boysenberry Ripple (page 42).

Rocky Road Sundae made from French Vanilla Ice Cream (page 12),
Chocolate Ice Cream (page 16), Hot Fudge Sauce (page 116), nuts and
marshmallows, garnished with a cherry and mint leaf.

Melon and Passionfruit Sorbet (page 73) and Tropical Sorbets with fruit garnish (page 79).

Plantation Parfait (page 52) and Tropical Sorbet Gâteau (page 76).

INDEX